"Loss is part of every life, yet rarely are we prepared for how to walk through the experience of grief and loss. In *Becoming Resilient*, Donna Gibbs takes us on a healthy and biblically anchored journey of understanding God's heart in the midst of our sorrow."

—**Tim Clinton**, American Association of Christian Counselors

"It's not a matter of *whether* we'll encounter difficulty in life; it's a matter of *when* and *how*. And even more important is how we respond. Donna Gibbs has helped many people get through rough seasons in life, and she shares a number of key concepts in this book to guide you toward becoming a more resilient person."

—**Greg Smalley**, vice president, Marriage and Family Formation, Focus on the Family

"Are you stuck in your 'Red Sea moments,' paralyzed and unable to navigate the tumultuous storms of life? *Becoming Resilient* offers practical, real-world steps from a fresh, biblical perspective not only to endure unique life struggles but also to triumph over them. Donna articulately and systematically empowers you to take on life's challenges with sincere gratitude and liberating resilience."

—**Lance Plyler**, MD, medical director, Division of World Medical Mission, Samaritan's Purse

"Donna Gibbs gives us a 'sain*'* les us to make suffering our frie in Christ Jesus, we are more tha va and let Donna's biblically ba

—**Dennis Swanberg**, agement

"Everyone goes through suffering at some point in their lives. How we handle that suffering is what moves us forward or keeps us stuck. Donna Gibbs gives us practical, biblical ways to move through suffering that we can use to enhance our lives and not let suffering destroy us. In short, she offers steps to developing resilience. Whether we have suffered trauma, sickness, or loss, we can become resilient by using the information Donna has shared in this great book."

—**Drs. Bev and Tom Rodgers**, counselors, speakers, authors, and founders of the Soul Healing Love Model of Relationships

"Donna vividly captures the emotional and spiritual trauma people suffer while living through a life-changing crisis. The real value of her writing is the examples of how people developed positive skills to work through these long days. She superbly combines the clinical findings from man with the biblical foundations from God. From these stories, the reader will gain a fresh perspective, a new path to recovery. . . . I highly recommend this book for anyone who is living through life's most challenging times."

—**Jeff Naber**, retired US Probation Officer

"Donna Gibbs does more than empathize with your hurts. She presents the real possibility for you to resiliently react to life's hurts. Her excellent research coupled with her own personal experience will help you rebound from what or who is overwhelming you. *Becoming Resilient* is a process that you will develop as you read this book. I highly recommend it!"

—**Dr. Greg Mathis**, senior pastor, Mud Creek Baptist Church

BECOMING
Resilient

BECOMING

Resilient

How to Move through Suffering and Come Back Stronger

DONNA GIBBS

Revell

a division of Baker Publishing Group
Grand Rapids, Michigan

Published by Revell
a division of Baker Publishing Group
P.O. Box 6287, Grand Rapids, MI 49516-6287
www.revellbooks.com

Printed in the United States of America

Library of Congress Cataloging-in-Publication Data is on file at the Library of Congress, Washington, DC.

ISBN 978-0-8007-2841-0

Unless otherwise indicated, Scripture quotations are from the Holy Bible, New International Version®. NIV®. Copyright © 1973, 1978, 1984, 2011 by Biblica, Inc.™ Used by permission of Zondervan. All rights reserved worldwide. www.zondervan.com

Scripture quotations labeled ESV are from The Holy Bible, English Standard Version® (ESV®), copyright © 2001 by Crossway, a publishing ministry of Good News Publishers. Used by permission. All rights reserved. ESV Text Edition: 2011

Scripture quotations labeled NKJV are from the New King James Version®. Copyright © 1982 by Thomas Nelson, Inc. Used by permission. All rights reserved.

Scripture quotations labeled NLT are from the *Holy Bible*, New Living Translation, copyright © 1996, 2004, 2015 by Tyndale House Foundation. Used by permission of Tyndale House Publishers, Inc., Carol Stream, Illinois 60188. All rights reserved.

Some of the names and details of the people and situations described in this book have been changed or presented in composite form in order to ensure the privacy of those with whom the author has worked.

In keeping with biblical principles of creation stewardship, Baker Publishing Group advocates the responsible use of our natural resources. As a member of the Green Press Initiative, our company uses recycled paper when possible. The text paper of this book is composed in part of post-consumer waste.

17 18 19 20 21 22 23   7 6 5 4 3 2 1

This book is dedicated
to all who are struggling.
Who are hurting.
Who are suffering.
I pray you will find hope
and healing in these pages.

CONTENTS

Contents

FOREWORD

Understanding and processing pain has been the topic of numerous books and sermons. Many authors and pastors focus on trying to understand why evil and tragedy exist if God is a loving God. Often, such theological questions leave the human heart feeling empty and confused, perhaps because God Himself said, "My thoughts are not your thoughts, neither are your ways my ways . . . as the heavens are higher than the earth, so are my ways higher than your ways and my thoughts than your thoughts" (Isa. 55:8–9).

I am convinced that we will never fully understand many of the painful and tragic experiences that come our way. That is why I was so encouraged when I read *Becoming Resilient*. This is not a book of platitudes. The focus is not on asking why tragedy happens but on how to have a healthy response to it. If tragedy consumes us, then two tragedies result. But if we embrace tragedy, then it becomes an event in our lives but does not destroy us. In fact, the tragedy propels us forward in choosing and living more purposeful lives.

Donna does not seek to cloak the reality of deep pain, but she does offer practical help on how to process pain in a healthy manner.

Through her journey as a counselor, she shares real-life illustrations of men and women who, through great tragedy, have deeply impacted the world for good. Living with an eternal perspective turns tragedy into ministry.

If you are walking through the valley of pain, this book will be a welcome companion.

Gary D. Chapman, PhD, author
of *The Five Love Languages*

Acknowledgments

I am eternally grateful to my heavenly Father. Were it not for His work in my life, I would have no truth or encouragement to share!

Thank you to my son Jordan, who randomly challenged me one day by saying, "Mom, isn't it time for you to write another book?" Little did he know I'd been wrestling with God regarding this manuscript for at least six months. Seriously, who wants to write about suffering? I am grateful that God gently uses others to spur us to submission!

Thank you to my husband, Mark, who prays daily for me and consistently encourages my obedience to God's call for my life.

Thank you, Dr. Gary Chapman, for your years of belief in and encouragement of my writing and for contributing the foreword for this book. I so appreciate your words of wisdom and support.

Thank you, Vicki Crumpton, executive editor at Revell, for seeing the value of this project and for providing great insights regarding the text. Traces of your feedback can be found throughout these pages.

I am also so grateful for the heroes introduced in this book and for the clients and staff of A Clear Word Counseling Center, in

Hendersonville, North Carolina. You are courageous champions. You inspire me, and you have taught me enormous lessons about life. Thank you so much!

And to you, the reader, thank you for joining me in this journey. I look forward to hearing about your victories. You are the reason for the book you are holding, and I am privileged that God has brought us together for this appointed time!

INTRODUCTION

Why?"

This is the shortest but most powerful question my clients ask. And I hear it nearly every day from those who are deep in suffering. This question is the earnest cry for some rationale behind the pain that nearly immobilizes. As a professional Christian counselor, I see people every day who are suffering. Really suffering. They are living the unbearable, the fullness of injustice, the worst of traumas, the heights of disappointments. They have experienced a depth of loss that cannot be calculated; and by the time they get to me, oftentimes they are drowning. Their world has stopped. They feel they are living outside themselves, looking at the unthinkable. On the good days, they go through the motions. On the bad days, they cannot function at all. If you are suffering, you know exactly what I am talking about.

I hear "Why?" from the mother whose husband was killed in a car accident as she struggles to understand how she will survive without him. I hear it from those who have been diagnosed with a challenging and chronic disease and wonder how their lives will change. I hear it from those who were physically or sexually abused as children and continue to live with the torment of the trauma into adulthood. I hear it from those who are persecuted and question why God would allow them to suffer unfairly at the hands of an enemy. I hear it from the father whose son was born with a birth defect that took his life. I hear it from someone who made decisions decades earlier that they now regret and can barely stand to verbalize. "Why?" may be the most common question we ask.

You may be the one posing the question right now. Perhaps you are facing the biggest mountain of your life. You have been given a hardship you don't think you can survive. You want to bounce back, but sometimes just getting out of bed is a task. I have met you—or at least someone like you. One at a time, I have talked to thousands of sufferers. They each took their spot on the soft plaid loveseat in my office. They bravely unfolded their story and at one point or another posed the question "Why?"

Early in my years of counseling, I was intimidated by that question. I am not a theologian, and I cannot unpack every Greek or Hebrew phrase in God's Word. I felt insecure trying to offer a theological response to a question a human being can never fully answer. You see, our real question is not "Why has God allowed this or that to occur in my life?" The underlying and most significant "Why?" of all is this: "Why would a loving, all-knowing, and all-powerful God allow evil to exist?" Evil summarizes the trauma, the pain, the death . . . the crux of all our suffering and pain. And we as Christians sometimes wonder why God allows the situations in our lives that take us to our knees.

I've studied God's Word as well as some great books that address suffering. I have come to the conclusion that God allows some suffering in our lives to expose the fullness of His character—His love and mercy, His compassion and concern, His forgiveness and redemption, His grace. In a perfect world, without suffering, we would never have the opportunity to experience the fullness of God. While this understanding is important, it will never fully answer the "Why?" of our specific trials. And it certainly is not sufficient in helping us *cope* during our suffering.

After nearly twenty years of counseling and serving in Christian ministry, I've encountered many who have narrowly, and sometimes destructively, survived their pain. If you are suffering today, all too aware of your weakness, you can learn to suffer well. You don't have to be a slave to inevitable struggles. In fact, you can learn healthy coping skills that will propel you to bounce back and even help you thrive. In the pages ahead, I am not going to try to simply explain why your suffering exists. Asking "Why?" creates an empty cycle of frustration that you have probably explored— unsuccessfully. "Why?" is the wrong question altogether and has possibly even lured you deeper into this pit you are screaming to exit. Instead of remaining stuck, we're going to learn to bounce back. Let's learn to live well when suffering is an inescapable part of life.

This book is a culmination of great truths I have learned from thousands of everyday people who have borne unthinkable pain and have trusted me amid their journey. They have taught me immeasurable amounts about how destructive we as humans can become when our pain paralyzes us. They have shown me how incredibly healthy and inspiring one who suffers well can be. Through disguised and composite stories in the chapters to follow, I'll introduce you to many of these people. You'll have the chance to learn from those who have been stuck and who have unintentionally developed disastrous methods of coping. You'll also meet some heroes who have built resilience and suffered well in the face of terrible circumstances.

You are about to encounter something different. No more wasting time exploring *why* you are suffering. You're going to discover how to survive—and how to survive well. You're going to learn to focus on the practical aspects of suffering, which will hopefully keep you off a plaid loveseat in an office that looks a lot like mine. "Why?" is not the only destructive question you'll learn about. A host of useless thoughts, questions, and coping skills are keeping you stuck. And, unfortunately, life can become much more challenging if those poor thought processes and coping skills aren't brought under control. So you're going to learn to bounce back by changing the way you think and adopting healthy skills that will transform the way you suffer.

Each chapter has a distinct purpose and flows somewhat like the counseling process. I assign homework for my clients; therefore, I will be assigning homework to you as well. At the end of each chapter, you will find a series of application questions. Take the time to consider them. This is where the rubber meets the road. Journal your thoughts. Talk with a trusted friend. These questions can foster real progress, and I don't want you to miss the victory that is ahead. If you are reading this book in a small group, use these questions to facilitate your time together. Each chapter ends with a victory verse. Grab hold of the truth in those words. Treasure them and repeat them often.

Each of us is sure to suffer at some point in our lives. Avoiding pain is not an option. Coping poorly in pain *is* an option, but one you will regret. I've seen sufferers transformed. I've seen those once debilitated by trauma become unstuck. Some of the healthiest people I know once sat in front of me on my plaid couch. They suffered the unthinkable and learned to suffer well. You can learn what they learned. Your story is not over. Let's work together in your journey to ensure that your story ends without regrets, without destruction, and without additional, unnecessary suffering. Let's learn how to build resilience when life's hurts try to keep you stuck.

Thanks for joining me. I've often said that I've been the most honored and blessed by those who have trusted me in their pain.

I look forward to hearing about the victories yet to unfold in your upcoming journey!

God, thank You for being ahead of us and with us. Help us discern the future journey. Give us the strength to endure. Allow this path to be productive, encouraging, and hopeful. Help us learn to suffer well. Amen.

PART 1

I'm Suffering . . . and I'm Stuck

If you've made it through the introduction and you're still with me, it's probably because you are struggling and genuinely desire some relief. Thanks for sticking with me and allowing me to guide you through this journey. I trust that God will bless your courage as you move forward.

To get us started, we are going to need to have some challenging, frank discussions. Part 1 is designed to aid us in those conversations. In chapter 1, we'll set a baseline for expectations of suffering. We're going to normalize the experience of suffering and identify different types and causes of suffering. Next, we'll bring to light specific destructive behavior patterns and poor coping skills that are keeping you stuck and potentially even causing you to experience additional, unnecessary suffering. We'll discuss what could happen if you remain stuck, as we explore the very serious vulnerabilities you may be experiencing. Woven through the first three chapters are compiled stories of individuals, just like you and me, who have stumbled in their struggles and have sometimes unintentionally made bad situations even worse. We'll look at why they stumbled and learn much-needed lessons from their journeys.

While the discussions in these first few chapters sometimes may be difficult for you, I encourage you to continue reading. Remember, God is faithful, and He will use our time in this first section to set the stage for your freedom. For your resilience.

I'm proud of you.

Now let's get serious about becoming resilient!

What Is Normal about Suffering?

Suffering. Pain. Distress. These are awful words. These are words we don't want to discuss. These are results of situations we'd like to escape. Yet each of us will face some form of suffering, for it is perhaps the most persistent of all human experiences. Suffering may be physical or emotional. It will be painful. Considering our culture, it makes all too much sense that suffering confuses us. Our economy is built on the desire for comfort, luxury, avoiding pain, and escaping difficulty. Money has minimized the experience and appearance of some of the suffering in America. Yet suffering continues. Though the wealthy are often buffered from some of the economic and social suffering faced by the poor, they are not immune to pain. Despite our best attempts and our most ingenious research, we all have seasons of physical, emotional, and/or spiritual suffering. Everyone experiences loss of some degree. Because we work so hard to insulate ourselves from problems, we struggle all the more when grief arrives at our door. And we rarely know how to respond when pain hits the lives of our neighbors, friends, or families.

What the Scriptures Say

Some popular preachers say that if you have enough faith, you will be protected from difficulty, and you will live a wealthy and prosperous life. This theology is simply not true. Here's what Scripture says about suffering.

Paul clearly writes in Romans 8:17 that suffering is a part of the Christian life: "Now if we are children, then we are heirs—heirs of God and co-heirs with Christ, if indeed we share in his sufferings in order that we may also share in his glory." For the early believers, and Paul himself, this sharing of suffering involved persecutions of all kinds—social, economic, and certainly physical.

James spoke of this challenge as well: "Consider it pure joy, my brothers and sisters, whenever you face trials of many kinds, because you know that the testing of your faith produces perseverance" (James 1:2–3). James encouraged believers to expect trouble in life. The Christian life does not promise prosperity; it actually promises struggle.

Solomon normalized seasons of pain, as recorded in Ecclesiastes 3:1–8:

> There is a time for everything,
> and a season for every activity under the heavens:
>
> a time to be born and a time to die,
> a time to plant and a time to uproot,
> a time to kill and a time to heal,
> a time to tear down and a time to build,
> a time to weep and a time to laugh,
> a time to mourn and a time to dance,
> a time to scatter stones and a time to gather them,
> a time to embrace and a time to refrain from embracing,
> a time to search and a time to give up,
> a time to keep and a time to throw away,
> a time to tear and a time to mend,

> a time to be silent and a time to speak,
>> a time to love and a time to hate,
> a time for war and a time for peace.

If we take these words at face value, we might think that roughly 50 percent of our "times" will be really difficult. Perhaps your seasons are not at a 50:50 ratio, but certainly you have experienced some challenging times. Solomon, in his wisdom, normalized the experience of pain that we, in this modern-day culture, work daily to deny.

We are introduced to the concept of pain and suffering early in the Scriptures. Oh, if only we lived in a pre–Genesis 3 world! Yet the events that transpired between chapters 1 and 3 set the world in motion toward disobedience and forever changed our experience of sorrow. When Adam and Eve failed to heed God's warning regarding the fruits of a particular tree in their perfect garden, God had to address their sin. Below is God's response to Adam and Eve, a response that you and I have inherited. It is this response that has determined the presence of anguish in your life and in mine:

> To the woman he said,

> "I will make your pains in childbearing very severe;
>> with painful labor you will give birth to children.
> Your desire will be for your husband,
>> and he will rule over you."

> To Adam he said, "Because you listened to your wife and
>> ate fruit from the tree about which I commanded you,
>> 'You must not eat from it,'

> Cursed is the ground because of you;
>> through painful toil you will eat food from it
>> all the days of your life.
> It will produce thorns and thistles for you,
>> and you will eat the plants of the field.

> By the sweat of your brow
>> you will eat your food
> until you return to the ground,
>> since from it you were taken;
> for dust you are
>> and to dust you will return." (Gen. 3:16–19)

God's response encompasses so much of the struggle you and I face so many years later. God was faithful in his assurance that childbirth would bring "very severe" pain. I can attest to that one myself! He shared the expectation that we would experience challenges in relationships that might create resentment and conflict. He warned that without work, we would go hungry, and that the work we would do would create anguish and difficulty. He instructed regarding the mortality of these bodies in which we abide. God did not sugarcoat or minimize the sentence placed on Adam and Eve. He was quite clear in His description of the distress that would characterize the experience of the human race.

Sources of Suffering

Some of the suffering we experience is inflicted by ourselves. Some is inflicted by others. Some suffering can be avoided, and some clearly cannot.

Our Sin

Some of our anguish, quite frankly, is the result of our choices. Sodom and Gomorrah is an obvious biblical example. The people of these cities disrespected God until their actions led to their demise. David, a man who loved God and whom God honored, suffered tremendously, oftentimes deep in despair, as a result of his sins. Jonah suffered a memorable detour in the belly of a large fish due to his disobedience of God's instruction. Suffering that results from our sin is often the most difficult to endure because it involves personal regret over once controllable and avoidable circumstances. Maybe you can identify because you are currently in misery due to the natural consequences of some of your choices. Perhaps you had an affair and now live alone because your marriage couldn't be reconciled. You fully realize that the grass really wasn't greener on the other side and earnestly desire to have your family back intact. You grieve because you realize that this reunion will never happen. Your spouse can't get beyond your sin, and you fear that your relationship with your children may forever be scarred. This type of loss is often more complex than a death, and you may sometimes find it difficult to get up in the morning or make it through your day.

Perhaps your story is a little different. Though few people know your real history, you are reminded daily that years ago you had an abortion. Your struggle is silent—one that few others are allowed to see. Your grief is deep and nothing eases your torment. Accepting forgiveness seems out of reach and perhaps even inappropriate in your mind. You suffer through your thoughts and memories.

Maybe you went to a seemingly innocent gathering one day and were unexpectedly introduced to heroin. Without thinking through the consequences, you decided to give it a try. This drug gave you an unanticipated escape from life's stressors. Before long, you became dependent on the drug, inviting some challenging people into your personal life and legal consequences that will follow you forever. You never set out to be an addict, but now you are a slave to a substance. You don't know how to cope with the physical symptoms you experience with withdrawal or how to get away from the horrible circumstances you have created. As it often is with suffering that we create ourselves, we are unaware of the subtle choices that generate our situations. As I often share with clients, sometimes "it becomes too late not to hurt."

Because of our sin or our destructive methods of coping with challenges, the ways in which we invite suffering into our lives are countless. In the chapters to follow, we are going to explore this aspect of suffering in more detail and strategize to ensure that we do not, from this point forward, invite unnecessary suffering into our lives.

The Sin of Others

We do not bring on all suffering ourselves (despite what some false theologians may say). Much suffering comes at the hands of others, through their selfishness, negligence, or, even more severely, their evil and criminal behavior. The most obvious biblical example of this form of suffering is Jesus—a perfectly innocent man who took on the sins of the world and suffered a horrific death at the hands of those who misplaced their anger.

Adolf Hitler was at the center of World War II and the Holocaust in Europe. Under Hitler's leadership, millions of Jewish men, women, and children as well as civilians and soldiers lost their lives. Droves of innocent people experienced severe abuse, humiliation, starvation, molestation, and annihilation. Their suffering was the result of the sin of other people.

The terrorist attacks of September 11, 2001, launched widespread fear and suffering in America. We as a nation felt the pains of vulnerability as well as the pains of loss on that terrible day—and continue to feel the effects to this day.

However, most suffering caused by others is not as publicly known as Hitler's regime or 9/11. I can't count the number of hours I've spent with victims of terrible childhood sexual abuse at the hands of someone they should have been able to trust. Their suffering may not be immediately apparent, but their pain is often so intense it is nearly tangible. If this is your story, your suffering is an emotional pain that can sometimes be relentless.

A drunk driver who crosses the yellow line and hits a car head-on brings suffering to an innocent party. The drunk driver may cause physical pain, or even death, in addition to residual emotional and psychological turmoil.

Physical and verbal abuse create affliction in the lives of those who are the targets of such abuse. Throughout my years as a counselor, I have worked with clients to develop a safety plan for them to escape their homes in case of a violent situation. No one should have to plan to flee their own home because of abuse! If these words trigger a tender spot in your soul, you too may have traumatic memories and carry a degree of hypervigilance and distrust that others can't possibly understand. You may even have self-hatred brought on by an abuser's destructive words.

Though these are just a few examples, you can probably already imagine how suffering caused by others can be difficult to process and often makes us vulnerable to destructive methods of coping. We're certainly going to spend some time in the coming chapters discerning how to process this pain productively and take steps toward healing.

Hurting at the Hands of God or Satan

We're especially reminded of our human fragility when we experience pain that is not caused by ourselves or anyone else around us. It is in our nature to place blame, and sometimes we find that the only two places to look are God and Satan. Sometimes we face a devastating diagnosis or a natural disaster and are humbled by our weakness as we suffer with the consequences of something that cannot be effectively controlled by any human being. When I consider a biblical example, I think of Hannah, whose sorrow and despair over her barrenness affected her so much that a priest thought she was drunk. Hannah was feeling an emptiness that seemed to be undeserved. And let's not forget Job, a righteous man who lost everyone he loved, every possession he owned, and even his physical health. He didn't bring this pain on himself, nor did any other human being. Job endured suffering as a result of a spiritual attack he could neither see nor understand. And remember the blind man described in John 9? In regard to his suffering, Jesus explained that "neither this man nor his parents sinned . . . but this happened so that the works of God might be displayed in him" (v. 3).

It's difficult to make sense of suffering that can't be blamed on someone or something else. This makes coping more challenging and sometimes causes us to become stuck in our anguish. We're going to discuss in the coming chapters how to cope when we truly have no control over preventing or managing the consequences of uninvited disappointment or disaster.

So, you see, suffering is a normal part of the human experience. Our world has seen evidence of pain since shortly after the beginning of creation. Brokenness is normal. Affliction is part of the human condition. If that were the end of the story, it would have a depressing and discouraging conclusion. Thanks be to God, it is not the end of the eternal story, and it is not the end of your story! The next chapter is vitally important because we are going to consider unhealthy responses to pain and how we find ourselves stuck in suffering. But first, make sure you spend some time reading the application questions below. Think and pray about your answers or possibly even discuss them with others. This will lay a strong foundation for the work to follow.

Victory Verse

There is a time for everything,
    and a season for every activity under the heavens.

Ecclesiastes 3:1

Application Questions

1. What are your reactions to the word *suffer*?

2. How have you been protected from pain as a result of living in America?

3. What did your family teach you about pain and suffering?

4. What have you grown to believe about suffering through the teachings of the church?

5. What are some of your personal experiences of suffering?

6. How have you experienced sorrow as a result of your sin?

7. How have you experienced sorrow as a result of the sin of someone else?

8. How have you experienced sorrow that has no reasonable cause?

9. Which source of suffering (self, others, God, or Satan) is the most challenging for you to accept?

10. What area of personal suffering do you most need to address in the chapters to follow? Where are you currently hurting and need some discernment or help?

Why Am I Stuck?

Tom works for a tree removal business that often involves him doing some risky climbing. He always knew the dangers of the job, but when he took a fall and was cut by a chainsaw, those dangers became all too real. Tom was rushed to the emergency room. He had a deep laceration and was bleeding profusely. The medical team's first step was to address the bleeding: it had to be stopped—and soon.

Hopefully, you have not fallen out of a tree and suffered a physical injury such as Tom's, but you may have an emotional injury that is threatening your well-being. You want to bounce back, but this injury has left you bleeding, and you need immediate attention.

Stop the Bleeding

When under pressure, we tend to regress to a certain mechanism of coping. As you read this chapter, be aware of your patterns. When you read an example that feels familiar, pay attention to how that particular coping skill has played out in your life and how it may have invited some additional difficulty somewhere along the way. We all require a coping mechanism, a safety valve of sorts. It's not the need for a coping skill that keeps us stuck; it's the choice of coping method. It's like the old phrase "Sink or swim." Some coping skills allow us to eventually thrive following a season of pain. Others cause us to sink. In counseling, one of the first steps is to identify those destructive coping skills. I call it "stopping the bleeding." As in an emergency situation, we have to locate the injury and place a tourniquet on it. Destructive coping skills are ineffective ways to stop the bleeding. These methods of coping keep us stuck in our pain and sometimes even threaten our lives. So let's identify the location of the injury and make preparations to stop the bleeding.

What Keeps Us Stuck in Suffering?

Simply put, *destructive patterns* and *poor coping skills* present a false sense of resilience, keep us stuck, and ultimately prevent us from bouncing back from life's hurts. Let's take a deeper look.

Destructive Patterns

Destructive Theology

I occasionally cringe when a client describes a conversation they have had with a friend or pastor. I've found that sometimes the other person, when offering guidance or instruction, omits either the full context of Scripture or the full context of the situation. Both omissions are dangerous. Such instruction is rooted in false theology and feeds false guilt. False guilt immobilizes. Let me share an example.

MaryAnn was tearful throughout my session with her. She carried multiple burdens, and my heart broke for her as she unfolded her story. MaryAnn had recently been diagnosed with breast cancer. She was the first in her family to have received this diagnosis, and she never saw it coming. We processed the normal range of emotions one faces when they hear an unexpected diagnosis. Unfortunately for MaryAnn, in an effort to seek spiritual support, she confided in her pastor from childhood as well as her parents. Their responses were nearly as surprising to her as the diagnosis itself, and she was rattled. They told MaryAnn that she was not exercising enough faith. If she had enough faith, she already would have been healed. They told her to consider any sins in her life that would have brought on this punishment. MaryAnn was broken.

She considered their words and adopted the belief that she had cancer because she had sinned and didn't have enough faith in God. She felt tremendous shame and mentally pored over every previous sin she could remember. She began to feel unworthy of God's love or help. She quit praying because she didn't feel God would want to hear from her. She quit going to church because she felt ashamed of the continued presence of cancer in her life. MaryAnn was suffering intensely, and much of her suffering was at the hands of destructive theology. MaryAnn's pastor and parents told her some powerful lies, and she believed them.

So what's the lesson here? God's Word is truth, and it is designed to free us. If Scripture is used to oppress others, then it is being misused. Considering Scripture without considering the full context of the Word is dangerous. Considering parts of a situation without knowing the entire context of the situation is also dangerous. Study the Scriptures yourself, and make sure that the counsel you are receiving from a friend or spiritual leader is consistent with God's truth, given the entire context of your situation.

Destructive Thinking

Name any negative emotion (fear, anger, jealousy, etc.), and I can guarantee a host of negative thoughts are also present. Negative thinking creates negative emotions. And negative emotions often create negative behaviors.

Carolyn is a beautiful young woman who came to me with a serious eating disorder called bulimia. Eating disorders are tough to battle because so much of the illness is deeply entrenched in the mind. After getting to know Carolyn, I discovered she had some destructive thoughts that had been initiated by a series of traumatic incidents in her life. We had to unfold Carolyn's beliefs. During our initial conversation, Carolyn revealed some destructive thoughts she had never disclosed to anyone else. "I am fat. I am ugly. I am disgusting. I am worthless," she said. "If I were skinny, others might like me. If people knew who I really was, they would not like me. I don't deserve anything good in my life. Others are better off when I am not around. I am scum. I am pathetic. I don't deserve people who can treat me nicely. I will not succeed in life. I want to die." As you can tell, Carolyn had many destructive thoughts, and they were repetitive. This harsh internal dialogue kept the bulimia alive and well. Carolyn was tormented by false beliefs, and they were creating a slow death by means of her bulimia.

So what can you take away from Carolyn's story? You may not be in the midst of a life-threatening eating disorder, but you may identify some destructive thoughts that hinder your freedom. We all have an internal dialogue, and it is either healthy and based on truth or peppered with false accusations, false assumptions, and false conclusions. Satan is an exaggerator and liar; his battleground is your mind. Dissect your internal dialogue to ensure that your self-talk is truthful, and then guard your healthy thoughts fiercely to prevent becoming stuck.

Poor Coping Skills

Asking the Wrong Question

I mentioned that asking why can be a bottomless pit and a quick trip to depression.

Mike's wife was killed a few years ago in a head-on collision on her way to work. Her death shook him to the core. He managed to survive the formalities in the days following her death, but he could barely function. This is a normal reaction to such devastating loss. The spouse who is left behind feels as though part of them died and sometimes functions as though they are only partially alive. Grief is hard, and asking why at some point is normal. I became concerned when Mike began repetitively *obsessing* about why his wife had been killed in the accident. He routinely cried out to God, focusing on why God allowed the accident. He couldn't fathom an acceptable answer. He drew out maps of the scene, interviewed every person he could find who was connected with the crash, and desperately sought to find some error that would rationally explain his immeasurable loss. While information gathering is healing for some individuals, and some degree of it is normal, Mike's obsession continued and distracted him from living in the present. He was suffering, indeed, but not suffering well. He sacrificed his job, his relationships with others, and even his ability to grieve because he focused all his energy on the wrong question—a question that would never be answered to his satisfaction.

Asking why is a totally predictable and normal thing to do in the midst of suffering. But when the question becomes a quest, it prevents us from suffering well and guarantees that we will become stuck. It keeps us wedged in the past, at the place where the specific suffering entered our lives. Focusing on answering this question is not likely to bring the closure we might be hoping for. Shifting from a destructive "Why?" to a healing "What now?" will help us to become unstuck.

Failing to Place an Appropriate Boundary

When we have had a physical injury, ensuring future safety is a priority in healing. We certainly don't want to reinjure a broken leg by putting ourselves in a situation in which it could likely be broken again. The same is true for an emotional wound. When we have experienced something traumatic that has introduced a new level of suffering into our lives, emotional safety is the first step. We must ensure that no additional trauma is added to the current crisis. I have noticed over the years that those who tend to get stuck in their suffering often fail to implement an appropriate boundary in some area of their life, as it relates to their struggle. Let me tell you about my friend Sandra. I think her story will feel familiar to some of you who are stuck.

Sandra had been in a long-distance relationship with a man for several years. She enjoyed their time together, as they liked the same types of activities. They traveled once every few months to spend some additional time together, and she fully expected that they would get married in the coming year. Then one of the man's friends, who felt the need to protect Sandra, revealed to her a shocking truth. Her boyfriend wasn't who he presented himself to be. He was dating other people, carrying on affairs with a couple of married women, at the same time he was proclaiming his love for Sandra. Sandra became severely depressed. She grieved her loss intensely, and this grieving was normal. I began to realize, however, that Sandra wasn't progressing through her grief in the way I had expected. I began probing for explanations, and I found the core of the issue. Sandra, still in love with her boyfriend, was far too tolerant of his insistence on contacting her. He texted or called every day. Sandra couldn't find the strength to block his number or change hers. Truth is, she was afraid to discontinue contact because doing so would solidify the reality that their relationship was over. I urged Sandra to discontinue contact. We needed to stop the bleeding. She had already decided she could never trust her boyfriend again and knew God was leading her away from him. But despite my urging and the conviction of the Holy Spirit, Sandra delayed setting this boundary. As a result,

she experienced unnecessary suffering and prolonged her healing process.

Boundaries are designed to ensure physical, emotional, and
spiritual safety. If you have failed to place an appropriate and
much-needed boundary in your life, then you are leaving the door
open for additional pain and almost guaranteeing that you will be
stuck in your suffering. Those with the gifts of mercy and compassion are most vulnerable to inadequate boundaries. The ability to
extend grace, turned up too high, causes some of the nicest people
in the world to be hurt over and over again. Remember, forgiveness
doesn't mean an absence of boundaries. A necessary boundary
prevents unnecessary suffering.

Obsession with Injustice

I've met with many people, men in particular, who have struggled with an unresolved injustice. They have suffered a clear offense,
yet there has been no punishment, no restitution, and no clear
justice. This lack of resolution feeds this person's anger, which
keeps them stuck in their suffering.

Daniel co-owned a business. He had been quite nervous about
the endeavor but felt it was time to take the risk. Daniel's partner
was enthusiastic and knowledgeable, which gave him confidence.
A couple of years into the venture, Daniel noticed that the profit
margin was slowly decreasing. After long hours of poring through
the details of various jobs, he realized that the company had some
undocumented profits. He could hardly believe it, but the only
explanation was that his partner was embezzling some of the
profits. Daniel sought the assistance of an accountant and, later,
an attorney. He pressed charges against his partner, but there was
not sufficient evidence to convict. Daniel was left without justice
. . . or money. He lost the company and was forced to file for
bankruptcy. Daniel began to exude emotional venom; he was so

furious that there was no justice in his situation. He couldn't even begin to consider forgiving his ex-partner and spent his waking and sleeping hours dreaming of how to make sure he was punished for the pain he had inflicted. Daniel was convinced that if he tried to work on forgiving his partner, he would somehow be condoning what happened. He refused to make progress. Daniel was miserable, and he began making those around him pretty miserable too.

It's easy to become fixated on the unfairness of the prosperity of someone who has wronged us. Often, we put our healing on hold, waiting for justice that may never come. We may find it difficult to move forward when there is unresolved injustice. It's important to remember that the bitterness associated with the obsession with injustice has little impact on the offender, but it is toxic to the person who is stuck.

Overanalyzing

Many people find that information helps them process their struggles. Once they have a few reasonable questions answered, they find it easier to begin to accept their painful situation and to progress forward. An analytical mind is a powerful strength, but when that gift is overused, it can easily lead to destruction. Overanalyzing is a perfect example of this type of destructive thinking.

Laura and her husband, Steve, struggled for several years with infertility. This was a painful journey for them, with the typical highs and lows of expectations and disappointments each month along the way. Naturally, their journey involved many medical appointments and learning more than they ever wanted to know about the reproductive system. Due to the many medical options and advancements in the field of reproductive endocrinology, Laura spent hour after hour researching. Her goal was to ensure that they were making a wise and godly decision about their treatment.

However, her desire to research began to take over her entire life. During dinnertime with her husband and during working hours when her time should have been focused on her job responsibilities, Laura had her head in the computer, desperate to make sure she didn't miss anything new that would affect their situation. When she wasn't looking at research, she was thinking it through in her head. She often contemplated the what-ifs and endlessly considered how she would feel or respond in various scenarios, most of which she never actually encountered. Laura was often preoccupied by her analyzing, and this distraction robbed her of being in the present with her husband and friends. Her quest for information began to cause a divide in her marriage, as her husband became jealous of the time she invested in her research and thoughts. What began as a reasonable and responsible journey for information turned into a quest that seemingly had no end, and it caused Laura unnecessary emotional turmoil.

When we face something difficult, some degree of analyzing is our responsibility and will potentially improve the situation. Excessively seeking information and overanalyzing that information, however, are distractions from healing and progress. Sometimes overanalyzing simply creates tunnel vision and serves as a tool for procrastination. It's important to pray about the amount of information needed to appropriately and adequately respond to a challenging situation—and beware of any overanalyzing that becomes destructive.

Overidentifying as a Victim

Victimization can occur through bullying, betrayal, physical or sexual abuse, fraud, gossip, favoritism, persecution, and the list could go on. Everyone has been a victim at some point and to some degree. We live in a sinful world, where oppression and selfishness are present. Not everyone who is victimized remains stuck. Those who overidentify with their victimization are vulnerable to becoming stuck in their suffering.

Vicki was sexually abused by her older cousin when she was a child. Her victimization was wrong, and it never should have happened. This was a difficult season for her, and she felt shame and confusion about what to do. When her parents found out about the abuse, they were devastated. They felt guilty that they had not recognized what was happening; they were tortured that they had not been able to protect their daughter. To compensate for the pain Vicki was experiencing, they began buying her lots of things and removed her rules and expectations. They tried to make life as easy as possible for Vicki. They would frequently remind her that they were making these changes because they felt sorrow for her. Vicki's parents saw her as a victim, and therefore she did too. Vicki began to see the abuse as a permanent mark on her. She no longer felt it was just a horrific experience. Now she began to feel it was her identity. She felt she was dirty and would be for the rest of her life. She felt unworthy of healthy relationships or the attention of a godly man. She had a difficult time trusting others, so she generally avoided letting others get close to her and guarded herself against being hurt. She felt her past prevented her from accomplishing certain things, so she didn't try. If confronted about a wrongdoing, she attributed it to her past. Her past seemed to dictate everything about her life. Vicki was immobilized by the abuse and stuck in her victimization.

Some traumatic experiences are so intense that they seemingly define us. Only time and really hard work can separate the experience from the person, but this distinction is crucial. The short-term *experience* of being a victim is different from the permanent *identity* of being a victim. Those of us who never make this distinction become stuck, sometimes for years. A perpetual sense of victimization creates a frequent reliving of the horrific event, which traumatizes again and again. Identifying as a victim often prevents us from setting and accomplishing goals. Defining ourselves as victims also may create negativity and depression as well as relationship problems (even abandonment), which further confirm the cycle of victimization.

Prolonged Denial

Grief will wait on us. Refusing to acknowledge loss or minimizing the impact of a loss will invite additional suffering. Though a degree of denial is to be expected, when denial becomes a familiar companion, we become stuck in our struggles. Maintaining prolonged denial eventually requires a destructive escape to keep the denial going and the pain at bay. The destructive escape becomes an additional problem that magnifies the loss.

Troy and his wife lost their child to SIDS. Their baby, Jeremiah, was only three months old at the time of his death. He had been the light of their lives, and they could hardly imagine living without him. The grief quickly became too overwhelming for Troy. To cope, he fell into denial. For the next two years, Troy avoided any discussion about baby Jeremiah. It was as if Jeremiah had never lived at all. He packed away Jeremiah's belongings and dodged anyone or anything that reminded him of his loss. He began working longer hours than required to escape being with his wife or in their home. The reminders were too much. Living as if Jeremiah had never been and as if Jeremiah had never died was easier for Troy than living in reality. Unfortunately, his attempt to feel less pain began to invite even more. His wife experienced additional suffering due to his emotional abandonment, and he nearly lost his marriage.

Denial is part of normal grieving. It is designed to be a short period of time in which we prepare to cope with a harsh and disappointing reality. When this short period of time turns into an extended one, we become emotionally weakened and unable to grow. If you are grieving, extend yourself grace for a short season of denial, but then begin leaning in to your grief as soon as you are able.

Tunnel Vision Catastrophizing

Amid a trial, it is our human tendency to fixate on the struggle right before us. When we face something traumatically painful, life seems to stop. Though temporary, a crisis can feel as though it is permanent. Unfortunately, this fixation often drowns out other important information in the "big picture" and can lead to greater anxiety and discouragement. In essence, tunnel vision has the capacity to keep us stuck if we hold on to a crisis too long and focus on it too intently.

Larry was laid off from his job. After eighteen years devoted to the same company, he never imagined he would receive a pink slip. In fact, he imagined that after giving them thirty years of service, he would retire from the company. He felt betrayed, but his struggle was more than just his feeling of betrayal. Larry began to fixate on the hurt and had a difficult time seeing beyond the layoff. He catastrophized his situation in his thoughts. "I'll never get another job," he'd often say. Or "Even if I get another job, I'll just be laid off again." Larry wasn't able to see that this layoff, as heartbreaking as it was, didn't have an impact on the permanence of his next job. Seeing this temporary transition as a chronic struggle caused Larry to become stuck. Rather than doing his best to embrace some of the benefits of his transition, Larry struggled with feelings of inadequacy and was fearful of his vulnerability in the job pursuit. He became depressed due to his tunnel vision catastrophizing and remained out of work longer than was probably necessary due to this difficulty in processing his transition.

We've all heard the phrase "The only constant in life is change." This is certainly true. We all experience both minor and major transitions, crises, and struggles in life. When we identify these times with permanence, we invite a heightened degree of suffering. A crisis naturally brings about an intense focus on the present, but prolonged tunnel vision becomes crippling. Allow the tunnel vision to alert you to your need to look at the big picture, and keep your focus there as best you can.

Unrealistic Expectations

Consider times when you've felt some resentment. You likely had certain expectations of a person or an experience, and things didn't play out the way you thought they would. When this happens, we grow angry and are vulnerable to becoming stuck in our pain.

Jessica was angry, and she was quickly growing bitter. She had just had her first baby and wanted to share this experience with her mother. To Jessica's surprise, her mom didn't come around very much. She stayed at the hospital only about ten minutes after the delivery and rarely checked on her after she came home from the hospital. Jessica became all too aware of the disconnection, and she was ticked. Years previously, Jessica had done some tough work dealing with her mom's years of selfishness. Her mother had abused drugs for several decades and had been in and out of her life. Her mom was finally clean, and Jessica expected that this new birth would change everything to the way it should have been all along. She thought her mom would be the kind of grandmother she saw in the pictures in parenting magazines. She expected that her mom would volunteer to help with the chores around the house. She expected that her mom would want to celebrate her grandchild. These things didn't happen. Jessica ruminated on what she felt her mom *should* have been doing and became so consumed with resentment that she could hardly enjoy her new baby herself.

Unmet expectations are often a result of *unrealistic* expectations. Our reluctance to reevaluate expectations is either because we don't realize we carry the expectations or because we don't want to grieve having to adjust the expectations. Though adjusting our unrealistic expectations is a painful process, if we do not do so, we will become stuck in our suffering.

Can You Identify?

As you read this chapter, you may have discovered that you are stuck in suffering. You may have identified with some of the stories I shared. You may be experiencing some of the specific stumbling blocks mentioned. Please do not be discouraged. This is an exciting discovery, and one God will use to begin breaking the shackles that have been restraining you! We all have an area of weakness that may be especially shaky when we're under duress. This area of weakness is often related to our background, our history, or our story. You are stuck because of a destructive pattern of behavior or a poor coping skill. You've likely relied on this pattern or coping skill at various times throughout the years. It may have kept you stuck in more than one struggle in your lifetime! You just need to replace this with something that will be more effective—and less oppressive. Now that you've identified the stumbling block, we must discern how to address it and "stop the bleeding." The prognosis will be unfavorable if this destructive pattern is not addressed. In the next chapter, we're going to take a sneak peek into just how destructive life can become if the bleeding isn't stopped. This next chapter will be a reality check of sorts, but it doesn't have to become *your* reality.

So keep reading. Keep praying! God is the perfect revealer of truth, and these revelations are designed to fuel growth. Sure, you're nervous. That's normal. You face an unknown ahead. But let's reframe that scary future you are thinking about into an awesome adventure. Let's reframe that discomfort as growing pains. God's been busy revealing truth. Let's get busy following Him!

Victory Verse

The Spirit of the Sovereign LORD is on me,
because the LORD has anointed me
to proclaim good news to the poor.
He has sent me to bind up the brokenhearted,
to proclaim freedom for the captives
and release from darkness for the prisoners.

Isaiah 61:1

Application Questions

1. Various patterns of destructive behavior or poor coping skills can potentially keep us stuck in our suffering. Sometimes these are easier to see in the lives of others than they are to recognize in our lives. Which ones have you seen in the lives of loved ones?

2. How have their destructive patterns or poor coping skills impacted their suffering?

3. Of the patterns of destructive behavior and poor coping skills discussed in this chapter, which are most common in your life?

4. How have these stumbling blocks kept you stuck?

5. Which person's story do you most relate to? Why? How can this connection be helpful for you?

6. Are you presently stuck in your suffering due to one of the destructive patterns or coping skills you've just studied? What evidence do you have of the presence of that particular stumbling block in your life?

7. What is your reaction to the discovery of the stumbling block in your life? How do you want to respond?

Why Staying Stuck Is Unhealthy

I'm just stuck. I don't know what to do." These were some of Sam's first words to me, his eyes looking down as if he were examining my rug. "I want to get beyond this, but I'm not able to do it."

Sam was stuck, all right. He had been presented with an unfair situation when he discovered his wife in an affair with his best friend. The affair had ended, and he felt his wife was now genuinely repentant. Sam desperately wanted to repair his marriage and felt convicted about his contributions to their relationship's vulnerability. He acknowledged that he wasn't the best listener. He could be quite critical. And he'd been working long hours for years, trying to climb the corporate ladder. He was ready to make some changes in these areas and felt his wife was absolutely committed to their future. If only he could get the images of her affair out of his mind . . . then he could work on their marriage. He went to bed with thoughts of the affair, and he woke up to thoughts of the affair. He felt tormented. He obsessively interrogated his wife throughout each day, asking questions that were no longer productive or healing. To cope with his obsessive thoughts and his wife's hurtful but honest answers to his questions, he had started drinking. One beer took some of the edge off. Several more stopped the obsessive thinking. A little alcohol created an escape, giving Sam slight relief from his pain. But a little alcohol had turned into a lot of alcohol.

Sam was suffering, but he was not suffering well. In fact, he was terribly stuck, and he was inviting additional, unnecessary suffering into his life. I felt the situation was urgent. If Sam didn't learn how to cope with his emotions in a healthy manner, he would soon lose all hope for a healthy marriage. His children, who were disgusted by his drunkenness, were already losing respect for him. He hated himself and was unhappy with the direction his life was going.

This is Sam's story—or at least the first part of it. Everyone has their own story and can recall times when they experienced some heartache and became stuck. We're all tempted into some form of destructive coping at one point or another. Why? Because even destructive coping still helps us cope. It's only later that we realize we have complicated our pain with our method of coping. Sam's story is a perfect example. The alcohol helped him cope. It *did* provide relief. He had no intention of creating more heartache or pain for himself—but that's exactly what happened.

A Challenge

Read this chapter with an open mind. If you notice any similarities to your life, reach out for help. Your destructive coping skills may have led to a stronghold, and you may need some assistance in discerning how to break free. A stronghold is something that has a grip on you. It controls you. At minimum, this chapter is a reality check meant to help you identify where your destructive coping skills can take you if left unbridled. Underline the content in this chapter that most relates to you, and then take this book to a trusted pastor or counselor to assist you in understanding why you are reaching out. Making that phone call or initiating that first tough conversation with a trusted confidant just might be the most courageous and life-altering action you've ever taken.

Residual Results of Remaining Stuck

Let's now discuss the residual results of *remaining* stuck in suffering. Suffering unleashed, without direction or boundaries, leads to absolute devastation. This list is not all-inclusive. Other tragic responses to being stuck exist, but these are the most common and the ones I'd like you to be most aware of.

Addiction

Sam never intended to become an alcoholic, but his pain escorted him there, and he didn't realize he needed to take a detour until it was too late. Sam, indeed, lost all that was dear to him and struggled through years of slavery to a drink that he eventually learned to loathe.

Addiction involves a persistent attachment to a substance or activity despite the presence of harmful consequences. Substances such as alcohol and prescription or street drugs are particularly enticing because they help the user escape their pain. In fact, they are *highly* effective in allowing the user to escape painful thoughts and emotions. If healing were this simple, I would recommend substances for everyone who is hurting. But healing is *not* this simple. Truth is, these substances are also highly physically addictive, and the user can easily become a slave to them before they even realize what's happening. What starts as a misguided desire to escape pain results in more pain than the user ever could have imagined. I'm sure you too have watched as someone lost everything and everyone important to them because of a raging addiction they never intended to invite into their life.

Addictions are not limited to substances. An addiction may also show up in the form of excessive shopping/spending, eating, cutting, internet usage/gaming, sex, or gambling. A person may become addicted to pornography, emotional affairs, one-night stands, or other sexual behaviors in an effort to escape discomfort for a moment. An addiction may even show up in seemingly productive areas, such as work, resulting in a person becoming a workaholic. *An addiction is anything that we attach ourselves to in an attempt to disconnect from pain and suffering. Addictions create significant additional suffering and cause us to be stuck in every way imaginable.* An addiction creates a false sense of escape, which, in reality, just creates another problem the person needs to break free from. If you are in the black hole of addiction today, then you must reach out for help. There is a way out, but it may be more than you can maneuver on your own. If you want to build resilience, you must address this trap first.

Unworthiness and False Guilt

When destructive theology, destructive thinking, and a painful trial collide, emotional disaster strikes. Our natural tendency in the face of pain is to look for somewhere we can place blame. This can be a painful pursuit. Sometimes no one is at fault. Sometimes the blame lies with someone we can't bear to admit was wrong. Oftentimes, blaming ourselves is simply easier, even when we may not be at fault. This false guilt can quickly become a chronic condition.

Let me describe a common example. Consider a child who just discovered that their parents are going to divorce. It's not uncommon for a child, in their efforts to make sense of what is happening, to assume they are at fault for their parents' divorce. They conclude, *If I'd been a better kid, this never would have happened.* They do extra chores in an attempt to become a perfect child at home, or they work feverishly at school to pull up their grades. They may try whenever possible to manipulate their parents into getting back together, but nothing they do is ever enough. They are left feeling as if they have failed. Unworthy. Deserving of punishment.

All of us carry on a private conversation within our minds. When false beliefs are left uncorrected, that private conversation becomes negative and repetitive. We call this rumination. When we ruminate on destructive thoughts, particularly those based on destructive theology, negative thinking becomes even easier to continue. Before we know it, we have very familiar, and entirely dangerous, automatic thoughts. Neurological experts now know that these automatic thoughts even have a detrimental impact on the brain itself. Our destructive thinking truly changes our brains over a period of time. We then make decisions based on our version of truth. We may settle for abusive relationships because we feel unworthy. We may isolate ourselves because we fear further abandonment. We may withdraw from challenges that are important to us because we fear failing. We may struggle with anxiety and depression. All as a direct result of our false guilt.

Sometimes guilt is in regard to legitimate sin and regret, but it becomes false when we linger in the guilt long after we have repented and God has provided forgiveness. When we feel bad about our previous choices and are hammered by our guilt, we will do most anything to alleviate our negative emotions. But guilt is not of God. Guilt is an endless, unproductive motivator. Conviction, however, is of God and is evidence of the work of the Holy Spirit in guiding us to start or stop a certain behavior. Once we respond to conviction, the conviction releases. We can try to respond to guilt, but the release never comes. False guilt is an endless, relentless bully that will live with us the remainder of our lives if we allow it.

Bitterness

Ever heard of the old phrase "Time heals all wounds"? I've discovered over the years that this phrase is simply not true. Time alone doesn't heal. That is why you and I both have met angry, bitter, grumpy, lonely, and . . . old . . . people.

Jana was divorced when she was only twenty-three years old, abandoned by her husband following his affair with another woman. Their child was only one year old at the time. Jana was devastated. She was also *extremely* angry. She was angry at her husband and angry at the woman whom she felt took her husband and destroyed her future. Years after the divorce, Jana continued to think about what happened. Not a day went by that she didn't remind herself of her husband's betrayal. She wanted so badly to get back at him so he would hurt just as she had hurt. For years, she spoke poorly of her ex-husband. She reminded her daughter often about the affair and the pain her ex had caused. When in public, she looked for opportunities to undermine his reputation. Jana was growing older, but no less bitter. Even more frustrating, her bitterness did not have the effect she wanted—she could never convince everyone that her ex-husband was a monster. In fact, people began confronting her—and then avoiding her. Her daughter severed their relationship when she became an adult because she had grown weary of the tug-of-war.

Jana was stuck in her bitterness, obsessed with the injustice of the affair, and didn't want to consider forgiveness. She had a false belief that her continued anger toward her ex-husband would somehow serve him with the punishment he deserved and prevent her from ever being hurt again. Her bitterness did nothing to punish him. Instead, it caused her to suffer even more. *Remember, when destructive coping skills are allowed to linger, they will invite additional, unnecessary suffering into our lives.*

Psychological and Emotional Challenges

When hit with a life-altering blow, we will experience some emotional challenges for a season as we come to terms with our new normal. That reaction is what post-trauma counselors often refer to as "a normal response to an abnormal situation." We are all human; therefore, we are going to experience a roller coaster of emotions during a season of suffering. However, an appropriate season of struggle is different from a lingering set of psychological and emotional challenges.

Sandra's older brother was killed in a car accident when he was seventeen years old. Sandra, who was fifteen at the time, was riding in the passenger seat. Her brother, a junior in high school, was driving them to school one morning when he ran off the road and struck a tree. He was killed instantly.

Sandra was the only witness to the horror of her brother's death and did not know how to handle her emotions. She wrestled with whether the accident was her fault—if she'd turned the music too loud or distracted him in some way. She felt incredibly guilty. She avoided being in a vehicle, fearful that the same thing would happen again. She fought repetitive images of her brother, lifeless, in the mangled car. She kept secret the tormenting flashbacks of the accident and often raged when triggered by anything that reminded her of her brother or the accident. Sandra felt she was going crazy, but she was afraid to let anyone know.

Sandra didn't understand that her immediate reactions were normal or that most people feel they are going crazy when they are in the initial stages of significant trauma and grief. This misunderstanding caused Sandra to isolate herself and begin living a very dark, inward, and lonely life. For the next several years, Sandra became a slave to her destructive thoughts. Depression became not just a short experience in her grieving process but more of a destination. She began physically cutting herself in an attempt to soften her emotional pain. Sandra eventually became so hopeless and defeated that she attempted suicide. She felt unworthy of living and just wanted the pain to stop.

Unfortunately, normal post-trauma reactions sometimes develop into post-traumatic stress disorder (PTSD), which leaves the individual in a heightened and prolonged state of hypervigilance and avoidance, making them vulnerable to anger, anxiety, depression, and general emotional instability. Being in a chronic fight-or-flight state causes the deep limbic system of the brain to become overworked, which leads to a negative neurological impact. Obviously, these patterns invite additional suffering and will likely require professional assistance to resolve.

You may not have characteristics of PTSD as Sandra did, but you may find yourself stuck for years, or even decades, in a pattern of psychological and emotional dysfunction. You may struggle with anxiety and panic attacks, depression, mood disorders, or personality disorders that negatively impact your daily functioning. If this describes you, then your suffering has taken its toll. It is possible to live a more stable life. Reach out for help, and do it soon, before your suffering steals any more precious time.

Manipulating or Giving Up

We live in a microwave-mentality culture. As a general rule, we have little patience. We want to see things happen. Now. Science and technology have advanced such that we do have a significant amount of control over many of our circumstances. Unfortunately, pain and suffering never comply with a timetable. When suffering is beyond our ability to control and doesn't resolve by the deadline we desire, our only choices are to manipulate, to give up, or to persevere. When married to unrealistic, microwave-mentality expectations, we are more likely to either manipulate or give up.

Think of Sarah and Abraham in the Old Testament. Despite God's promise that they would have offspring, Sarah could see only her infertility. She had tunnel vision, and God's promise was not unfolding in a timetable that was acceptable to her. She felt she couldn't persevere, but she didn't want to give up. So she journeyed into one of the most memorable examples of manipulation in Scripture. Sarah arranged for Abraham to get her maidservant, Hagar, pregnant, and, boy, did she make a mess out of things! Sarah's decision caused conflict, turmoil, and abuse in her relationship with Hagar. Marital dissension and resentment between her and Abraham soon followed. Ishmael, the son of Abraham and Hagar, brought additional strife. Sarah hated the results of her manipulation, and she complicated her suffering tremendously.

Maybe you aren't tempted to use manipulation. You may feel you don't even have the *energy* to manipulate. Whether due to an unexpected and life-altering medical diagnosis or the devastation of a broken marriage, you may be inclined to wave the white flag. As a result of lingering destructive patterns and coping skills, you don't want to embrace the hard work that would be necessary to overcome your situation. You reason that there is no guarantee things will improve anyway. You give up too fast, quickening the anguish you will experience, when perhaps work could still be done to reduce your suffering.

When discouragement hits, we easily grow weary. *Suffering never resolves as quickly as we'd like.* Whether a battle is physical or emotional, we will feel as though we're swimming upstream when attempting to address our situation, and we don't have the strength to persevere. It just feels too hard. Too overwhelming.

Maybe it's just not worth it. Many times we give up prematurely because we have expectations of a doomed future. In giving up too soon, we miss out on some wonderful rewards that often follow perseverance.

Physical Illness

God made us whole. That means when one part of our being struggles, it causes a ripple effect, and other parts of our being also struggle. For instance, when we have the stomach flu, we may also feel discouraged. Or, if we have heart disease, we may also be vulnerable to depression. The reverse can also be true. An emotional or spiritual pain can bleed into our physical well-being. When we are chronically stuck and emotionally unhealthy, we are also more vulnerable to physical illness.

The fascinating book *Deadly Emotions*, written by Dr. Don Colbert, references this mind-body connection. Dr. Colbert writes, "I am thoroughly convinced that the body absorbs stormy emotions, and if they remain there, they set in motion a series of biochemical reactions that eventually end in disease."[1] He reviews the scientific evidence behind his conclusions regarding the connection between our physical, emotional, and spiritual struggles. Our unresolved pain and inability to bounce back from life's hurts truly make us vulnerable to being sick and trigger the disease process. If you struggle with physical illness today, I encourage you to consider the impact your unresolved emotional pain is having on your physical body.

Addictive Suffering with Help-Rejecting Complaining

Sometimes our struggles, our victimization, and our suffering become the most familiar components of our lives. Depression, shame, anxiety, bitterness, grief, sickness, and addiction become weirdly comfortable and predictable after a period of time. So much so that we have a hard time imagining life without pain. We even become afraid of life without struggle. This may seem very odd to you . . . unless you are addicted to your suffering. If that is the case, then you can readily identify with the familiarity that brings complacency and stagnation. Pain has become a part of your routine, your explanation for inadequacies. It consumes your time and attention, even your identity. You may be afraid of resilience. You may be afraid of bouncing back. You may wonder, Who will I be without the struggle? What will others expect of me? What will I do with my time? What is my purpose, apart from pain? Any unknown creates angst, and when we are addicted to our suffering, we become very much afraid of change. This fear leads to behaviors that sabotage our resilience and keep us stuck.

These behaviors can be described as help-rejecting complaining. Oftentimes, taking specific, clear steps will alleviate suffering and allow us to become unstuck. When those steps are rejected and the complaining persists, then help-rejecting complaining immobilizes and ensures that suffering will continue.

We often don't even realize we are stuck in this pattern, but those around us will know, because they may grow quite frustrated with our insistence on remaining stuck, no matter what they do to try to help. Help-rejecting complaining will never help us climb out of a pit in which we are stuck and will only leave us more lonely in that very pit. One by one, those who have been the cheerleaders and encouragers will grow weary having their offers to help rejected, and they will eventually stop offering. Once again, our destructive coping skills will have invited additional, unnecessary suffering.

Eating Disorders

I have a special place in my heart for those who struggle with eating disorders. In fact, a significant portion of my caseload is dedicated to addressing anorexia, bulimia, and binge-eating disorders. What almost all of my clients who suffer from these disorders have in common is self-loathing, distorted body image, destructive thinking, and depression. Many who struggle have been victimized or controlled in some manner during their lifetimes, and their emotional pain is intense. An eating disorder is a false sense of resilience, a deceptive black hole filled with promises that will never come to pass. Recently, a client who is in partial remission wrote an anonymous letter to be given to others who are blinded by their struggle. Below is a portion of that letter. Her words are a window into the darkness that is bulimia.

Hey,

You don't know me, but I know you. I know you very well. I know the pain you feel, the hurt you have, and the depths of despair and darkness that surround you. There's this voice telling you you're not worth it, you'll never be worth it, you don't deserve worth the way you are. Your eating disorder tells you in order to have worth, success, acceptance, love, and control, you have to do what it says. It hurts you. It forces you to hurt yourself. It makes you cry and purge and eat and purge and cry. It tells you this is the way to get what you truly want.

But what it doesn't tell you is that it hates you. It hates you so much it convinces you to hate yourself. This voice doesn't want you to succeed. It wants to kill and destroy everything you have ever held dear. It will take everything from you. Your family, friends, job, grades. Your happiness, excitement, wonder, curiosity, attention, time. It will thin your hair, destroy your teeth, and weaken your fingernails. It will strain your heart, destroy your esophagus, and wreak havoc on your digestive system. But, ultimately, it will take your life. It won't just physically kill you; it will emotionally and mentally destroy you first until you just want to die. It will become all-consuming. Until you eat, breathe, sleep bulimia. It will become the only thing you care about, the only thing on your mind. Nothing else will matter. Every time you purge, you flush away so much more than food. You flush away your life. You flush away any chance at true happiness. Every time you purge, you fall deeper and deeper into the lie. Into the black hole that is bulimia. This black hole will suck you in and utterly destroy you. There is no such thing as happiness in an eating disorder. Only death.

If you read this and can relate to the belief system my client describes in her letter—the obsession with bulimia (or any other eating disorder), the thoughts of worthlessness—please let someone know. You have probably worked hard to keep this a secret, but you have become a slave to an unworthy master. Help is available. The promises of the eating disorder are empty, but you can have a hope that is rich and full of life! Reach out today. I promise you, a way out is available and you are worth it.

Spiritual Disconnect

If you are stuck, then you are also probably feeling disconnected from God. You may feel He has abandoned you. Or maybe you've chosen to abandon Him because you no longer believe He has the power to intervene in your life. You may feel He doesn't care or that He is against you instead of for you. You may go to church and find it stale and routine. You may read Scripture and feel it is dry. You may be really angry. God, who promised His ways are not intended to be harmful, has allowed something horrendous to enter your life. You may feel betrayed by Him. At minimum, you may be disappointed in His protection.

A season of spiritual struggle following a loss or a tragedy or a disappointment in life is normal. We have a relationship with God, and that relationship naturally will be stronger at certain times than others. However, when we become stuck due to destructive theology or thinking, we are vulnerable to a chronic disconnect. You see, God is a gentleman, so He is not forceful. When we want our space, He allows it. Unfortunately, our struggle can become our primary focus. We don't intend to worship our suffering, but when we become stuck, we unintentionally become excessively devoted to it. This excessive devotion may develop into a form of unintentional idolatry that has prolonged a normal period of spiritual struggle into a long-term disconnection from God.

One thing is for sure—God desires you, whether or not you feel He does. He is the greatest source of your resilience, and this disconnect must be addressed for you to bounce back from the hurts that have kept you stuck. Bridging the disconnect will require risk. You may feel you can't trust God anymore. You may be afraid of what He will do with your faith in Him or your pursuit of that relationship. I encourage you to lean in to that unknown.

Cry Out

After thinking through the long-term effects of destructive coping skills, I am reminded of times in which King David became stuck and invited additional suffering into his life. Often, in the Psalms, we see him cry out to God in anguish and desperation. Let's follow his lead and cry out to God today. Talk with Him about what you have discovered after reading the last two chapters. Lay out your mess before Him. Allow yourself to be vulnerable and transparent. Invite God into a discussion about the areas of your life that you may have previously prohibited Him from entering. What do you have to lose?

I'm looking forward to the remainder of this journey. The following chapters will show you ways to get unstuck. To bounce back. To build resilience! Let's get started!

Victory Verse

You, God, are my God,
  earnestly I seek you;
I thirst for you,
  my whole being longs for you,
in a dry and parched land
  where there is no water.

Psalm 63:1

Application Questions

This chapter covers some heavy topics. The discussion of what reality could look like if you stay stuck certainly serves as a reality check.

1. What thoughts and feelings did you have while reading this chapter?

2. Though other tragic responses to being stuck exist, this chapter addresses some of the most common ones. Do you notice a personal vulnerability to any of these responses? If so, which ones?

3. If any of the struggles mentioned in this chapter are present in your life, then you are undoubtedly experiencing additional

suffering beyond the initial struggle that made you vulnerable. What additional suffering has this brought into your life?

4. Remaining stuck has cost you something or possibly someone. List below specifically how it has robbed you:

5. Share any discoveries from this chapter, along with your list above, with someone you trust.

PART 2

Getting Unstuck . . . Building Resilience

I f any of the discussions in the previous chapters resonate with you, then it is time for a serious heart-to-heart. Be honest. Is previous trauma/pain/loss holding you back? Is previous trauma/pain/loss chronically and destructively impacting your emotional well-being? Your physical well-being? Your decision-making? Your relationships? Do you have dark thoughts? Are you sitting at home with the blinds drawn, hoping your life will somehow be shortened so you can escape your misery? Are you motivated by guilt? Do you have thoughts of worthlessness? Do you struggle with drugs or alcohol, though you never intended for them to become your master? Do you struggle with an eating disorder? Do you find yourself rejecting practical help from those who love you? Are you becoming awkwardly comfortable with your pain? Do you feel disconnected from God? Are you bitter?

If you can answer yes to any of these questions, then you are not simply carrying the results of your initial suffering; you are now also carrying the additional, unnecessary suffering that is a direct result of being stuck. It is dangerous to be stuck. It is not as simple as prolonging pain. Being stuck is a direct invitation to additional pain. Being stuck costs you. Being stuck robs you. Being stuck should make you angry!

When I was a child, one of my favorite things to do was to walk behind my grandmother's house and play in a small creek that flowed through a grove of trees. I enjoyed wading in the clear water, searching for creatures. I'd see tadpoles, lots of worms, and occasionally even a small fish. On a few occasions, my excitement was trampled by the discovery that the creek was stagnant. Have you ever seen a foul, messy creek? It's gross. It smells. It's dark and muddy. And not one living creature is nearby. On those occasions, I'd work to clean up the creek by removing branches and leaves so that it could begin flowing freely again. Cleaning up took some energy, but it was the only way to bring life back to the creek I so enjoyed.

Your life may sometimes seem similar to that stagnant creek; you may feel as if you have lost the joy and zeal for life you once had. You desperately need something that can come in and clean up the creek that is your life, and anger may be part of the solution. You may initially think of anger as a sinful emotion and feel guilty about feeling angry. But let's look at anger from another perspective. Scripture doesn't identify anger as sin. Ephesians 4:26 warns: "In your anger do not sin." This verse identifies anger as something that can *lead* to sin if it is allowed to control us. Anger is a powerful emotion. In fact, anger is the most productive emotion we feel, which is also why it can be challenging to manage and can easily cause us to sin. When used inappropriately, anger will destroy people and places. But when used righteously, anger can be the perfect fuel for our resilience. That's right! God, who made us in His image, created us with the capacity to feel anger. God created within us an emotion that can lead us out of our oppression. So let's appropriately direct this powerful emotion toward whatever is keeping us stuck, whether it is destructive theology, destructive thinking, or a destructive coping skill. God can use anger to clear the stagnant creeks of our lives. I challenge you, then, to allow appropriately directed anger to build some momentum that can be used to help you begin bouncing back from the hurts that have kept you stuck.

Resilience is sounding better and better, isn't it? The remainder of this book is devoted to helping you use appropriately directed anger and the tools we will discuss in the coming chapters to take some specific steps in bouncing back. It's time to replace that all-too-common "Why?" with a new and refreshing "What now?" Ask yourself, *What do I need to do to make sure I survive this storm? What do I need to learn to ensure that I thrive in this struggle? How will I build resilience?*

I'm excited, and I hope you are too!

Acknowledge the Suffering

Baby Jessica was only eighteen months old when she fell twenty-two feet into an abandoned dry well in Midland, Texas. It was a morning like any other as little Jessica played with other children at the day care center owned by her aunt. But around 9:30 a.m. on October 15, 1987, Baby Jessica took a fall that would suddenly invite suffering into her life. You may remember hearing this story on the news. Rescue workers lowered a microphone into the well so they could hear Baby Jessica. "She is crying, she is humming, she is singing," reported Sgt. Jeff Haile.[1] Rescue workers worked diligently around the clock to burrow through rock to get to this little girl who was stuck in a literal pit of suffering.

What if there had been no rescue effort? Baby Jessica was stuck and incapable of getting herself out of the well. She was deep in darkness, with seemingly no way out.

Truth is, we all have the option of staying stuck in our suffering. Even when we are stuck in an unavoidable situation (as is the case of chronic or terminal illness or an unresolved trauma), we can choose how we respond. And we don't have to settle for a further paralyzing reaction. Without rescue, Jessica would have perished. Without intentional work to become unstuck, we may also perish in a physical, emotional, or spiritual sense.

What a model little Jessica is for all of us. Just a toddler, she showed us how to suffer well. "She is crying. She is humming. She is singing." Suffering naturally brings pain, fear, struggle, and even crying. Little Jessica cried because it was her instinctive way of expressing her suffering. In fact, as a young toddler who could have probably communicated only a handful of words, crying was perhaps her *only* method of conveying her pain and fear. But Jessica also hummed. And she sang. She even slept at one point in the midst of the recovery effort. Jessica was immobilized in a deep well, but at the age of only eighteen months, she modeled for us how to bounce back from life's hurts.

Moving beyond Denial

Isn't it interesting how children are unrestricted? A toddler doesn't mind taking off their clothes and playing naked in the middle of the living room. They lavishly display their love for someone. They can dramatically display their dislike as well! When it comes to suffering, they are never in denial, and they are forthright in acknowledging sadness. They waste no time. They've not yet developed destructive coping skills that will hinder their ability to bounce back from their struggles. So much can be learned from God's youngest children!

We talked in chapter 2 about prolonged denial and its ability to arrest us at the point that suffering enters our lives. Healthy denial is designed to be a short-term coping skill that allows us to absorb and survive a brand-new, painful reality. Denial is not designed to prevent us from living in reality long term, but that is exactly what happens when our fear urges us to camp out in denial longer than necessary or helpful. So let's look at how we can move beyond denial and acknowledge our suffering in a healthy, nonthreatening way. Acknowledgment is important because it brings our suppressed struggle from the subconscious to the conscious mind. In our conscious mind, thoughts, emotions, and behaviors that were once subconscious reactions to a denied reality can now be reprocessed in a healthy way and better understood. Once we understand the connections between our suffering, our thoughts, our emotions, and our behaviors, we are in a position to make intentional changes toward growth. This beautiful transformation begins with our first step: acknowledging our suffering. This step facilitates an amazing journey in gaining freedom and resilience.

Let's take a peek at what this step looks like for someone who is suffering. I want to introduce you to some of my heroes in suffering: people who have faced tremendous pain, trauma, and loss and have developed some skills in bouncing back. I know you'll be inspired by their courage and their resilience.

Laura

I met Laura when she was in a desperate place, on the brink of losing her job, her marriage, and her very self. She was on the verge of a breakdown, and deep pain was the root cause. Laura had been keeping a secret for nearly ten years and felt she was about to lose control of that secret. When Laura was a freshman in college, she became pregnant. She was in shock. She was terrified. She told her boyfriend and then her parents. Their reactions were entirely unexpected and almost equally as shocking as the pregnancy itself. They all agreed she must have an abortion and that the pregnancy never would be spoken of again. Still in shock, Laura was easily influenced by the unanimous pressure to abort

71

the baby, so she proceeded with their plans. Just as promised, the baby was never mentioned again.

Laura lived in a secret prison, avoiding anything related to abortions or unnecessary reminders of this dark and confusing time in her life. She built a tremendous emotional wall around herself that allowed no one to discover the secret that was growing more difficult to hide. Finally, as she sat before me, it became clear that she had been tormented by this pressured decision for many years, and she had deep, unresolved remorse regarding the loss of her baby. In the ten years since the abortion, she had not once uttered the word abortion. But she said it that day in my office. And she began to acknowledge the pain and regret that had dominated her life for many years. We discussed the power the enemy had over her. You see, Satan has increased leverage with our pain when it is kept hidden through silence and denial.

Let's not gloss over the pain here. Acknowledging the abortion was perhaps the most painful admission of Laura's life. She vomited periodically throughout this discussion, as it was so painful that it made her physically sick. You see, truth does set us free, but rarely is it comfortable in the initial stage. That discomfort is precisely why we stay in denial too long. We want to avoid the process of exposing truth and acknowledging exactly what we have experienced. We don't want to cry. We don't want to experience such intense pain that we become physically sick. We fear reliving the trauma. We fear losing control. Ultimately, we fear losing our minds. But in continuing to avoid the truth, we miss out on the rewards of taking the risk.

Laura came back to me a few weeks later a different person. Yes, she still had many challenging issues to face, but she was no longer bullied by the abortion. Though she had sought God's forgiveness years previously, for the first time she now felt she had *accepted* His forgiveness and could audibly say the word *abortion* without becoming physically sick. She smiled with relief that a burden she'd struggled to carry had been lifted from her, and she felt free to deal with other tough issues she needed to address. Laura told me she had kept a secret wish for years—that someone would tell her what was wrong with her. With this painful experience acknowledged, she began to better understand her unpredictable emotions, her behaviors, and their connection to her painful past. Her secret wish was answered. Laura was beginning a beautiful process of building emotional stability and resilience, and it began with acknowledging her suffering! She was no longer stuck. She was free to begin the process of bouncing back from the hurts that had immobilized her for almost a decade.

Laura didn't begin to build resilience until years after this tragic event. She had been stuck at the point where the suffering began. She suffered additional, unnecessary pain as a result of being stuck. This also caused her recovery to be more complex, which was unfortunate. Let me be clear: you don't have to suffer for years before you can begin building resilience. Maybe a life-altering struggle has just entered your life. Don't postpone healing. Begin the tough work of building resilience now! Don't wait until you have invited additional suffering. The pain will wait on you, so denial will do nothing to help. Let me share a story regarding one of my heroes, a former colleague in ministry who leaned in to his suffering *without* delay.

Mark

Mark was diagnosed with leukemia as a teenage boy. He faced months of isolation as a result of a bone marrow transplant in an out-of-state hospital before the interactive benefits of the World Wide Web. During that trial, his body was broken so that it could be preserved. Mark miraculously survived that experience and afterward followed God's clear call on his life into ministry. Since that experience, Mark has had special connections with people young and old who have suffered a harsh diagnosis, and he's never been shy about telling his story.

Three years ago, I received a call from Mark, who described his expectation that he would soon receive another dim diagnosis. A couple of weeks later, while he was serving in short-term missions in Africa, that diagnosis was indeed confirmed. This time the diagnosis was male breast cancer. Mark embraced the rare diagnosis. He spoke of it to God, without hesitation. He spoke of it to others around him, without hesitation. He called it what it was: male breast cancer. He wore his pink shirts and posed in photos with female survivors of breast cancer. He joined with other breast cancer advocates, boldly sharing his story when his body would permit. Each week through the journey, he blogged his physical, emotional, and spiritual struggles through social media. He didn't minimize his diagnosis or his suffering. Nor did he minimize his God and all that he was learning through the journey. Mark is an absolute inspiration. Why? Because he hastened to embrace, to the best of his human ability, whatever pain God allowed him to experience. He acknowledged his suffering, not only to God but to others as well, which allowed him to bounce back from the suffering that could have easily kept him stuck. Mark is an incredibly resilient individual. We're going to hear more tips on building resilience from Mark in the pages to come.

How to Acknowledge Suffering

You may be thinking, *That sounds great, but how do I acknowledge my suffering? What does that look like?* So let's get practical. Acknowledging your pain just means you call it what it is. Don't back away from using the words that best identify your experience. If it was rape, call it rape. If it is cancer, call it cancer. If it was suicide, call it suicide. If it is infertility, call it infertility. If it was an affair, call it an affair. Acknowledge your suffering now, and acknowledge it accurately. Call it precisely what it is or what it was. Don't sugarcoat it. Don't excuse it. Don't minimize it. Don't exaggerate it. Be honest. Speak of the emotional impact. If you're discouraged, say it. If you're sad, admit it. If you're heartbroken, acknowledge it. If you're scared, verbalize it. No, this doesn't mean you have to rehash every graphic detail. This is not designed to be punishment. Quite the contrary.

Everyone is different, so naturally some people prefer certain methods of acknowledgment over others. Some may literally speak out loud and acknowledge their suffering in the privacy of their homes or on the top of a secluded mountain. Some may prefer to process their acknowledgment with a trusted friend, pastor, or counselor. Others may journal. Some may write a letter to an offender. (I do not recommend sending these letters without first consulting with a counselor. Oftentimes, sending a letter is unproductive or even counterproductive.)

For an acknowledgment to be effective, you must speak it to yourself and speak it to God. God may or may not lead you to also confidentially acknowledge your suffering to another person. If He does, then trust that He will help you and obey His urging.

What can you expect? Yes, you will probably cry. Yes, it will probably hurt. I say often in counseling, "It is too late for it not to hurt." In a rare case, you may even become physically sick. You've taken a tough blow. Similar to when you take off a Band-Aid, you're going to feel the sting. But the sting will diminish. The grief of the acknowledgment will subside, and when it does, it will open the door for you to begin to bounce back. Once the pain is acknowledged, you will find some relief, some hope. You need this step to begin building resilience, so prepare now to take this risk.

We're going to talk a lot more about this in the next chapter, but it is important to say now that there must be a "Yes, but . . ." following our acknowledgment of suffering. We must tell the whole story. I just introduced you to my friend Mark, who learned he had male breast cancer while in Africa. He told his Ugandan friend about the diagnosis, and she gave him a "Yes, but . . ." that stuck with him through his suffering. Her prayer following Mark's acknowledgment was, "God, what is cancer compared to You!" What a beautiful example of a "Yes, but . . ." We can fully acknowledge our suffering while also fully acknowledging our God. What a significant balance in building resilience!

So acknowledge your struggles, but keep them balanced with the rest of the story. We're going to discuss much, much more about this important tool in the next chapter.

Double Whammy

One of my heroes of the Bible is Hannah. We learn of her suffering in 1 Samuel 1. Hannah didn't experience a *simple* struggle, or even a *single* struggle, yet she is a model for how to acknowledge suffering appropriately and build the resilience necessary to bounce back from life's hurts.

Hannah had what I refer to as a "double whammy"—two major pains that caused her to suffer, each of which would have been painful enough on its own. Issue #1: Hannah's husband (Elkanah) was also married to another woman (Peninnah). You heard me right, there was another woman! Issue #2: Hannah was unable to have a child in a culture that based a woman's value on her fertility. To complicate matters even more, Peninnah was a cruel bully who, year after year, provoked and made fun of Hannah because she was barren. We know Hannah suffered, because the Scriptures say that when she was taunted by Peninnah, "Hannah would be reduced to tears and would not even eat" (1 Sam. 1:7 NLT).

You may already be able to relate to Hannah. Perhaps you are accustomed to crying or know what it is like to be so grief-stricken that you lose your appetite. Maybe you too are suffering because your husband has "another woman," and you are tormented by her unwelcomed presence. You think you can't compete with her, and you feel such intense betrayal that you can't formulate words to adequately express your pain.

Perhaps you can relate to Hannah's long-suffering battle of infertility. I personally know the pains of childlessness, as my husband and I were married for eight years before we had children. As Hannah did, we too would pray and plead with sorrowful hearts and were often confused by God's silence. Hannah probably wondered why God would allow a mean-spirited person such as Peninnah to be blessed with children, while she sat alone with empty arms.

Maybe you can directly relate to one of Hannah's two specific issues. Maybe you can't. But you can certainly relate to heartache, so it's important to see what can be learned from Hannah's experience. Hannah had some secrets to suffering well. It is clear that she suffered, but it is also clear that she did not get stuck. Let's take a peek at some evidence of her secrets. According to 1 Samuel 1:9, Hannah went to the tabernacle to pray. She leaned in to her suffering. She went to the tabernacle clearly intending to express her sorrow to God. She is recorded as having been very distraught. She was crying. In fact, according to verse 10, she "was in deep anguish, crying bitterly as she prayed to the LORD" (NLT). Her suffering could not be hidden. It was visibly and audibly evident. Hannah acknowledged her intense grief to God. She was very specific in expressing her pain, her loss, and her desires. She didn't hold back. Her acknowledgment was so powerful that it even confused the priest, who sat in the back of the tabernacle and witnessed her acknowledgment. "As she was praying to the LORD, Eli watched her. Seeing her lips moving but hearing no sound, he thought she had been drinking" (vv. 12–13 NLT). Have you ever been so honest with God, and so grief-stricken, that you couldn't even formulate words or put sentences together? Have you ever suffered to the point that you could only mumble your words, with the hope that God could decipher the rest? Hannah was at that same point of deep pain.

Any bystander would have thought that Hannah was drunk. In fact, Eli was offended that she had entered the tabernacle in such a seemingly drunken state. Eli's confrontation opened a door for another confession. Hannah admitted her struggle to Eli. Much as she had to God, she confessed to Eli the deep despair she had been feeling. "I haven't been drinking wine or anything stronger. But I am very discouraged, and I was pouring out my heart to the LORD. Don't think I am a wicked woman! For I have been praying out of great anguish and sorrow" (vv. 15–16 NLT). Hannah acknowledged her suffering to God and to Eli. She bravely and honestly identified her pain, her emotions. We don't know if Hannah had ever been in denial prior to this encounter, but these few moments of honesty clearly were incredibly significant in her healing.

So what happened after Hannah acknowledged her suffering? Did she have a panic attack? Did she crumble in tears? Did she become even more depressed? Thankfully, Scripture tells us more about what happened that day.

Hannah did not leave the tabernacle crying. She wasn't stuck. She wasn't bitter. In fact, "She went back and began to eat again, and she was no longer sad" (v. 18 NLT). She gained something at the moment of her acknowledgment. That something was hope! Though she undoubtedly experienced complex and deep despair, Hannah never gave up. She didn't try to hide, minimize, or suppress her pain, and she called it precisely what it was. She prayed an earnest prayer of acknowledgment, and this step paved the way for relief from the emotions that were oppressing her so intensely. I think Hannah also had a "Yes, but . . ." experience in the tabernacle, don't you? She left with a fresh perspective that came from a balance of her acknowledgment of raw suffering and her acknowledgment of a loving, powerful, and purposeful God.

The Great Exchange

One of my favorite Bible verses comes from the New Testament: "Come to me, all you who are weary and burdened, and I will give you rest" (Matt. 11:28). If you have faced an uninvited tragedy, disappointment, diagnosis, or loss, then you have been burdened. You are tired. You might be downright exhausted. You are weighed down. "Come to me" are the sincere words of a gentle Savior, inviting you to seek safety and rest in Him. Your weariness qualifies you for this invitation. He desires that you acknowledge whatever it is that oppresses you. And in return, He offers rest and peace and relief. I call this the Great Exchange. Meditate on this Scripture passage. Close your eyes and imagine the scene. Jesus is standing with arms open wide. He is pursuing you. He invites you to express your burden. And then to lay it down at his feet. Imagine Jesus taking your burden and handing it to the Father, then returning to you as His arms become a bed of rest for your exhausted soul. He knows your struggle, and He offers help and hope for the pains that are crippling you. Acknowledge your pain to Him. Respond to His invitation. This step frees you to begin the work of building resilience and prevents you from being stuck in your suffering. True, confession of sin is good for the soul. But so is confession of suffering!

> *Victory Verse*
>
> Come to me, all you who are weary and burdened, and I will give you rest.
>
> Matthew 11:28

Application Questions

1. Denial arrests us at the point where suffering enters our lives. Have you experienced denial regarding your struggles? How has this complicated your recovery?

2. It is normal to have fears about confessing our struggles—this is the very thing that often keeps us in denial. What specific fears do you have regarding acknowledging your suffering?

3. Sometimes it is difficult to formulate our words. We saw this with Hannah, who could only murmur inaudible words in the tabernacle. Because of this challenge, it can often be helpful to write down our acknowledgment. I challenge you to do this and then continue to answer the questions below. (If you don't feel comfortable writing your acknowledgment down in a place where others might later find it, simply write it down on a piece of paper and then shred or burn it. The process of writing it down is still important.)

4. Sometimes writing things down, getting them out of our heads and onto paper, allows us to see a situation, loss, or trauma in a light we have never before noticed. What did you discover about the hurt you have experienced, or its impact on you, as a result of writing it down?

5. Laura's acknowledgment of suppressed pain allowed her to better understand herself, her emotions, and her actions. What have you grown to better understand about yourself through this process?

6. Now that you have your acknowledgment of suffering written down, you are more prepared to approach God confidently and boldly with your pain. Read your letter to Him in the form of a prayer. Admit your pain to Him. He has invited you to come to Him. Now invite Him to come to you.

7. Pray about the possibility of sharing your experience with someone you trust. Those who bounce back from life's hurts most effectively are typically those who are willing to share and admit their struggles with someone they trust. It is certainly not necessary, nor is it recommended, to broadcast your suffering on every corner, but acknowledging your pain to another mature Christian friend, counselor, or pastor is often helpful.

8. Now that you've acknowledged your pain, what is your "Yes, but . . ."? Write it below and make sure that whenever you ponder your struggles, you also add this most important aspect of your suffering!

Tell the Whole Story

Ray was broken and overwhelmed. His wife of seven years, Jana, had recently committed suicide. Now a single dad, Ray was left with two young children to raise. He was also emotionally tormented by events surrounding Jana's suicide. They had been separated for a while, and she wanted them to get back together. Ray was the last person Jana called prior to ending her life. He felt horribly guilty about what happened, and the harassing insults from her family accusing him of being a murderer were not helping matters. He was beginning to wonder if he would be able to survive this tragedy. Ray was stuck. And, boy, was he suffering!

As I would do with anyone affected by a suicide, I guided Ray to "tell the whole story." This, of course, can be challenging in regard to a death. We feel guilty about acknowledging anything that would potentially shed a negative light on the deceased, who aren't there to defend themselves. But as I told Ray, I've come to understand over the years that a suicide is never an isolated event. There is always more to the story. There is a history. A vulnerability.

And often complex family dynamics can potentially create a guilt-inducing blame game.

Telling the whole story is an invitation for God to shine light on truth. It's not a time for false flattery. It's not a time for exaggeration. Instead, it's a time for exposing important facts that contribute to our struggles. Acknowledging all the facts is a vulnerable process. Why? Because sometimes it just feels easier to focus on certain aspects of our pain. Sometimes it's easier to accept blame, even when it is not ours to accept, because placing the blame on someone else may require another level of grieving. However, because we can hardly stomach our own contributions to our suffering, sometimes falsely blaming someone else is easier. We're already hurting so badly that we just want the pain to stop—and we're afraid of complicating things.

Partial Facts Lead to Partial Healing

I've discovered over the years that partial facts lead to partial healing. Telling the whole story exposes either a denial of responsibility or a weight of false guilt and allows for honesty about our suffering and our situation. When we're stuck in suffering, we may hesitate to face all the details of our situation. Sometimes we want to deny the details altogether. Sometimes we want to water them down. Sometimes we focus on a few facts and ignore many other significant ones. Sometimes some of the facts seem too difficult to consider. Exposing the *whole* story, though strenuous, brings clarity to the situation and frees us from being stuck. Yes, raw pain is hard to focus on. But we do so for a purpose.

For Ray, telling the whole story meant fully acknowledging that Jana's suicide was not an isolated event. It meant honestly discussing why he had asked her for a separation months previously. He disclosed that, though Jana's family refused to acknowledge it, she was addicted to alcohol and had also had numerous affairs with other men. Ray had hoped the separation would inspire her to get some much-needed help for her addiction. He also assumed it would be a wake-up call regarding the affairs that were destroying their marriage. But that's not what happened. Even during the separation, Jana continued to struggle with alcohol addiction and remained in a relationship with another man. Despite her refusal to change her ways, she persistently asked Ray to reconcile. He knew he couldn't bring her back home. He also knew she was depressed, but he hadn't expected her to commit suicide.

Ray came to recognize that Jana had already been making a series of irrational decisions, and the alcohol made her even more vulnerable and less inhibited regarding the decision to commit suicide. Ray had to acknowledge that, though he had not been a perfect husband, he never wanted the separation. Jana's destructive choices forced his hand in the matter. He also never desired her death, nor did he take conscious steps to promote it. The separation simply acted as a necessary boundary for his own protection and that of his children. Jana, in a poor mental state, decided to take her own life. It was necessary that Ray give his wife full ownership of that particular decision for him to begin the steps to becoming healthy again. Ray also had to acknowledge that Jana's family had been in denial for some time regarding her struggles. Therefore, it was unrealistic to expect them to be understanding and supportive of him after her suicide. They were devastated themselves and obviously not able or willing to acknowledge the whole story.

Ray was thrust into a new normal that he never invited. If he was going to remain sane and build the resilience necessary to survive this unthinkable trauma, then he would have to invite God to shine light on truth and acknowledge all the facts.

Telling the whole story opened the door of healing for Ray. Obviously, this doesn't mean Ray bounced back to exactly how things were before. And he never will. But it does mean Ray embraced a new normal, and he continues to grow healthier and more resilient each day.

A, B, C, and D

I remember having a conversation with a friend of mine who trains law enforcement all around the world in lie detection. He explained that the best liars actually tell the truth. They don't commit lies or falsify testimony; they simply omit important truths. "Let's say I'm investigating someone and they tell me facts regarding A, B, and D. They are not lying to me about A, B, and D. But I have to find out the facts regarding C. The best liars are just those who omit C." The same could be true when we are stuck in our suffering. We may be lying to ourselves because we focus only on partial facts. Yes, we acknowledge A, B, and D. But the full acknowledgment of C is vital to our healing. Remember, partial facts lead to partial healing. To build resilience and bounce back from life's hurts, we must be willing to tell the whole truth.

Scott

Scott's story is very different from Ray's. Scott was one of my husband's roommates in college. A great guy. A guy who just didn't seem deserving of the suffering that would come his way in the years that followed our carefree college experiences. But suffering did come. And it came in multiples. Scott married the love of his life, Sarah. They were happy newlyweds, reveling in all the excitement and infatuation that accompany that stage of marriage. Scott was spiritually grounded and had married the woman he knew God had led him to marry. In fact, he had always felt that Sarah made him a better man and inspired him to godliness. So you can imagine his utter devastation when, only six months after their wedding, they were in a car accident that would change Scott's future. While driving on a slick, unfamiliar road on a rainy day, Scott lost control of their vehicle. After the crushing impact from hitting the end of a bridge abutment, their car was hurled over the bridge and quickly became submerged. Under the muddy waters, Scott wrestled to break free from his seat belt so he could get to Sarah. He fought and fought to free his wife from the mangled vehicle. Soon bystanders and EMS joined him in a desperate but unsuccessful attempt to save her life.

I've asked Scott to share some of his thoughts about that experience:

I cannot describe the loneliness, fear, anger, guilt, and pain I felt that day and for many weeks and months after. God and I had some serious discussions and arguments, though it was mostly me doing the talking. I could not understand why He would take the only woman I had ever loved—after only six months of marriage. Why didn't He take both of us? Or just take me instead? I would have preferred either of those options. But through all those terrible days, I never once felt that He had left me. I hated what happened and made that clear to God. He simply allowed me to ask the "why" question continuously, even though the full answer did not come. He continually whispered the words of Psalm 46:10 into my soul: "Be still, and know that I am God."

God did not give me all the answers in the days and months to follow. But He did give me peace and comfort when no one else could. I remember driving back from the graveside the day we buried Sarah and asking why for the thousandth time. Did God realize when He took her home to heaven that He also took a piece of me? Did He realize I could never be the same? That day I heard Him speak to me like at no other time in my life. It was not an audible voice, but it was definitely His Spirit speaking to my soul. It answered my questions as if to say, "*Yes, that is true, but* I left a part of her in you as well." That comforted me greatly. It gave me the peace I needed. I knew, as Paul writes in 1 Thessalonians 4:13, that we "do not grieve like the rest of mankind, who have no hope." I knew I would see Sarah again one day. I still didn't completely understand, but He showed me how He used Sarah to shape me to be more like Jesus. He told me I still had things left to do.

Perhaps without even realizing it, Scott utilized a few important coping skills early on in his suffering that prevented him from getting stuck. First, he was never afraid to acknowledge his suffering. He spent hours crying out to God with brutal honesty. Sure, he asked why. But notice that he chose to focus his attention on God's "Yes, but . . ." response. Aren't you glad God originated that response? Without fail, when we come to Him in our distress, He draws near with a yes. He validates and comforts us. He closely attends to us when we are brokenhearted. But He also nudges us, through the Holy Spirit, to recognize that there is something more to the story. There is hope. Thankfully, Scott allowed God to guide him in acknowledging that God had more planned for him. And it's a good thing he did, because Scott would endure even more tragedy in the few years following Sarah's death, and he would need a healthy foundation.

Scott eventually married a wonderful, beautiful, and godly woman. Just as with Sarah, Scott felt that God had brought Monica into his life. A woman who loved him, made him a better man, and challenged him to be more like Jesus. After some time, they were overjoyed when they found out that Monica was pregnant. Unfortunately, little Abigail, whose name meant "father's joy," was born with an extremely rare genetic condition called Treacher collins syndrome, in which some bones and tissues in the face are not developed, and neurological and respiratory difficulties can arise. This syndrome is typically not life-threatening, but it certainly provides challenges and promises future surgeries.

Abigail had to be fed with a gastrostomy tube. When she was only five months old, her feeding pump was hooked up just as it had been each night since her birth. At some point during the night, Abigail spit up while sleeping on her back, causing her to aspirate. Her body was lifeless before her parents realized what had happened. According to Scott, "I don't know for sure, but I think it happened minutes before I entered her room. One minute? Five? Ten? I don't know, but it was so painful to think if only I had been awoken a little earlier. If only . . . The thought tore me up for a long, long time."

Red Sea Moments

Two unthinkable tragedies. Isn't this too much for one young man to face? Scott refers to these two tragedies as his "Red Sea moments." By that, he means markers in time in which God brought him through difficulty and demonstrated His love and faithfulness, just as He did for the Jews when they fled Egypt and Pharaoh. Though our trials may be difficult, sad, and painful, we come out of Red Sea moments with a new and stronger faith. "Christ didn't calm these two Red Sea moments in my life, but He held me closer than I've ever felt and calmed me in a way that now seems impossible," says Scott. "Just as Moses sang his song of praise in Exodus 15 after the Israelites crossed the Red Sea, I have my own song of praise to sing to God."

What If?

Scott's suffering, as terrible as it was, was not as profound as God's work in his life. What would have happened if Scott hadn't acknowledged all the facts regarding his traumatic losses? What if he had just focused on the fact that he was driving the car? Or that he couldn't get his wife out of the mangled vehicle? Or that he had walked into

Abigail's room only moments after she had aspirated? What if he had been unwilling to consider these trials as his Red Sea moments? What if he had not recognized God's closeness because his focus was exclusively on his loss? What if he had felt that the spiritual intimacy was less important than the tragedy? He would have unquestionably been emotionally and spiritually *crippled* his entire life. He would have been entirely vulnerable to the many struggles we discussed earlier. I can assure you he would not have lived well in his suffering. He would have added additional, unnecessary suffering to the unimaginable pain he was already enduring. I am grateful Scott didn't fall into that trap. He was willing to tell the whole story not only to us who read it but also to God and to himself.

Cindy

Cindy was sexually abused by a family member when she was a young child. And, like so many other abused girls, she spent years thinking of herself as dirty, worthless, and undeserving. You see, her offender drilled certain thoughts and beliefs into her head, and she lived with this belief system as her reality for many years. Her emotions, her relationships, her decisions, her physical appearance—everything about her was tainted by this experience, and she was stuck. The reason? Because she focused on only part of the story. She focused on what her offender falsely instructed her to believe. Like the bodies of many who are sexually abused, her body sometimes became aroused. *How could my body experience any kind of pleasure in something so detestable?* she wondered. This created a level of false shame that sealed the deal and made it impossible for her to acknowledge other important facts. Because of this tunnel vision, she could not imagine being anything other than "worthless trash."

What is the rest of her story? And why are those facts necessary to her building resilience? Cindy's offender was decades older than her. Like many offenders, he told her his actions were her fault and that she was causing him to hurt her. Other times, he would convince her this was normal in families and was a part of showing love. He routinely threatened that her family would be split up if she told anyone. He was obviously a predator, though Cindy had never seen him as anyone other than a relative. She had never dealt with the facts regarding him. She had never acknowledged the whole story.

She also needed to acknowledge some important facts about her body. The fact that her body became aroused didn't mean she wanted the abuse to happen. Her body was designed to experience pleasure when touched in certain areas. She couldn't help the fact that the context for the touching was completely and utterly wrong. All these facts combined to create massive confusion and shame for a young girl who never should have been exposed to such pain. Cindy had to consider these experiences in light of physiological facts.

Most important, Cindy had to compare the things her offender had told her about herself with who God proclaimed her to be. Never before had she considered those truths. Cindy had been dealing with partial "facts" from someone who routinely lied to keep her under his power.

For Cindy to begin building resilience, she had to tell the whole story. Understand that this didn't mean she had to share every detail of her abuse. But it did mean she had to acknowledge that she had been a powerless young girl fighting against a manipulative, evil, and much stronger man. It also meant she had to challenge the beliefs she had always had about herself and the situation, because her entire belief system was based on partial truths.

An Intimidating Experience

Telling the whole story can be intimidating. It opens an unknown that we naturally fear will grow beyond our control. I'll be honest with you. God's revealing of truth is not typically a comfortable experience. In the beginning, it makes us pretty squeamish. Though our partial facts have paralyzed us in many ways, they have also served as the backdrop for a familiar way of thinking and responding. Altering the backdrop of our lives can naturally create some anxiety. Here's an even more important truth: when we alter the backdrop, *it can create some resilience*! Our new normal is healthier and safer. So if you are anxious about telling the whole story, know that your feelings are normal. Anxiety feeds off the unknown, and this is unfamiliar territory for you. However, if you want to be resilient, you must face the unfamiliar and acknowledge hidden but significant facts.

I mentioned earlier that when we are stuck, telling the whole story exposes either a denial of responsibility or a weight of false guilt. Let's talk a little more about these two discoveries.

Denial of Responsibility

If you have been struggling and know you are stuck, then consider the possibility that you may need to recognize some significant aspects of your story. To help you accomplish this challenge, contemplate the following questions. Do you need to stop denying an area of sin that is adding additional suffering? Are you stuck because you have failed to take responsibility for your actions? Do you need to seek the forgiveness of God and/or others? If so, then this is an important part of your story. And until you address it and assume responsibility, you will remain stuck.

Weight of False Guilt

If you realize today that you are stuck because of the weight of false guilt, then it is certainly time to tell the whole story. No, that doesn't mean you have to tell others your story, though that can certainly be helpful. But it does mean you have to tell yourself the whole story. Lying to yourself by refusing to acknowledge significant details can cause you to be hindered by guilt and stuck in your suffering. You may be assuming responsibility for something that was not your fault. Or you may simply be leaving out important facts regarding your situation that could be giving you peace and hope. Remember, partial truths lead to partial healing. Fill in the gaps. Tell the story, and tell it completely.

Taking a Different Perspective

If your suffering is the direct result of someone else's sin, then telling the whole story must also include looking at the situation from the perspective of your offender. Let me preface this by saying that this should not be done in an attempt to excuse their behavior. Absolutely not. We are each responsible and accountable for our sin, and this person has created pain in you that never should have been. But telling the whole story, including the perspective of your offender, will aid you in moving beyond your pain and building resilience.

Specifically, ask some questions about your offender. What is their history/background? What are their vulnerabilities/fears? Where have they been hurt? What might have been their thoughts regarding the situation? What were they up against? Did they intend to harm you? If they did have intent to harm, what would it be like to live with that mentality? Have they faced challenging consequences as a result of their actions? Put yourself in their shoes to the extent that you can. It is even okay to feel sorrow for them. This in no way excuses the hurt they caused you. You are simply identifying them as a sinful human being who has wounded other people. Just like you and me. Although their offense may be hideous and nothing short of evil, they are a broken and lost soul, hopeless and lonely in their dark world, and perhaps hopeless in eternity.

I know this is a stretch. You may even be angry right now at the prospect of considering the struggles of your offender. However, having empathy for an offender, though not required, is often a facilitator of forgiveness. And forgiveness propels resilience. So despite the fact that this discussion may seem offensive to you, it is truly in your best interest. You may have some hurts you need to release. Your offender may have far too much control over your life as a result of your unwillingness to let them go. If you find this angle of your story challenging, I encourage you to engage the help of a professional who can further aid you in assessing your wounds and processing your feelings.

How to Tell the Whole Story

Telling the whole story is a biblical tool. When we tell the whole story, we are not doing it alone. We are doing it with Christ. So ask Jesus to shine Himself on your story. Ask Him to speak the full truth about your story. Jesus is Light: "I am the Light of the world. Whoever follows me will not walk in darkness, but will have the light of life" (John 8:12). Therefore, when you invite Him into your story, He shines light on darkness, and He reveals truth. In that revealing, you have freedom.

That freedom can help you begin telling yourself your whole story. Start by simply thinking about it in totality, writing out some thoughts if necessary. You may decide to have a conversation with a friend or family member. If you find yourself struggling, it may be that you need the assistance of a pastor or counselor. Oftentimes, we are so caught up in our own stories that we can't see what is under our noses. Bringing in a third party who can see things objectively will be a great help in your telling the whole story.

Most important, you will need to have a conversation with God about the facts. When God exposes truth, it begins to facilitate change and the building of resilience. Even good change requires some work. Some stretching. Some risk. But the results are transforming. Hold on, because soon the discomfort will subside and the oppression will begin to lift. Remember, you've invited Jesus into the scene of your suffering, and there is no darkness or oppression in Him! With light shining on darkness, there is hope!

One Last Thought

Let me offer one last thought regarding the importance of telling the whole story. We've just talked about Jesus, who is Light. But what if we focused on only part of *His* story? What if we covered nearly every detail regarding Jesus: His birth in simple surroundings, His time growing up with His family, His early years of teaching, His baptism, His calling of the disciples. What if we even told the events of His crucifixion, but then we stopped? Without the rest of the story, Jesus would be just a dead prophet. We would have no hope. We would be eternally stuck in suffering. But the story of Christ contains one more significant event that simply can't be left out—the resurrection. It changes everything. It means Jesus is alive. He is powerful. His hope is real. His promises are legit.

So, today, face the facts. With Jesus on your side, shining light on darkness and revealing truth, reveal the whole story of your suffering. What facts have you hesitated to acknowledge? How do they change things? Remember, like telling about the crucifixion while leaving out the resurrection, sometimes just one detail changes everything!

Victory Verse

Guide me in your truth and teach me,
for you are God my Savior,
and my hope is in you all day long.
Psalm 25:5

Application Questions

1. Consider a painful area of your life. What aspects of that story do you routinely think about? If these are partial facts, what is the rest of the story? How do these additional details change things? What fears do you have about telling the whole story?

2. What have been some Red Sea moments in your life (times in which you have experienced God's closeness most profoundly)? What did you learn from those past experiences that can help you now?

3. When you ponder your struggles, do you typically focus on the painful circumstances? Or do you balance your story with thoughts regarding your experiences of God's closeness?

4. Telling the whole story generally exposes a denial of responsibility or a weight of false guilt. Do you recognize either of these patterns in your life after reading this chapter? If so, how has following this pattern previously kept you stuck in your suffering?

5. If your suffering is a result of the actions of another person, then looking at the situation from their perspective, which aids in empathy, can assist in forgiveness. What is your reaction to considering the perspective of your offender?

6. Though their sinful actions are without excuse, do you desire to forgive and release your offender?

7. After reading this chapter and thinking about your story, what thoughts of hope do you have?

Consider a Different Angle

I live in a household of male sports fanatics. Ask about almost any statistic related to college or pro basketball and someone in my home can probably answer it. I am always amused by their reactions to a close call in a game. They obnoxiously burst from their seats and rush toward the television. But then they quickly quiet one another as they await the replay. Specifically, they want to see the shots from different cameras. Each camera on the court provides a different angle and gives more information about what actually happened in the play.

Photographers have long known that a shift in perspective changes things. A different angle can transform a simple image into a work of art. Something as ordinary as a few blades of grass, captured at just the right angle, can be breathtakingly beautiful.

Recently, in an effort to better childproof my home, I learned a lesson about perspective firsthand. To gain the perspective of a toddler so that I would know what areas of my home needed to be addressed, I decided to spend a little time on the floor. I was struck by how different—and large—everything seemed from the floor! I was looking at the house I live in every day, but it appeared vastly different. Now imagine if I'd taken the time to get a view of my home from Google Earth. I'd have the ability to see the same home from three radically different angles that provide three radically different perspectives.

So it is with life's hurts. We sometimes need to see situations from a different perspective. Why? Because as often is the case with a televised basketball game, we don't always see things as they really are. In life, we tend to see only the things that fit through our filter of beliefs and experiences. We have a narrow scope, and this tunnel vision tends to keep us stuck. We don't take in everything that is true about a situation unless we choose to do so intentionally. When it comes to hurts in life, we must be intentional about viewing our situations from a different angle and training our minds to expose a new way of thinking. The result? Resilience!

Embracing Gratitude from a Fresh Perspective

"Your best-case scenario is that you will be here for a long time. Not weeks but months. If your length of stay is any less than that, then it means things didn't end well. With that said, you are going to have to put into place, for yourself, every tool you've ever used as a counselor. We can't afford for you to get depressed." These were the solemn words spoken to me by my physician, who came by my bedside in the early days of a three-month-long hospital stay. He spoke frankly regarding the seriousness of my condition. He also spoke firmly about the necessity of my emotional and spiritual resilience, despite the circumstances.

I took those words very seriously. Because of my work as a counselor, I was well aware of the connection between the physical, the emotional, and the spiritual. I also knew I was up against the most significant physical trial of my life, and the only way to get through would be with emotional and spiritual fortitude. I reflected on 2 Timothy 1:7: "For God has not given us a spirit of fear, but of power and of love and of a sound mind" (NKJV). I knew God had put within me the ability to maintain a sound mind, despite my hardship. So I did exactly what my physician prescribed: I used every tool that I recommend for others, and I refused to let depression take even a foothold in my life. Every tool you see in this book I utilized myself during that season of struggle. I found particular value in looking at my situation from a different angle. Rather than focusing on my physical suffering or the length of my trial, I forced myself to consider other aspects of my trial and find gratitude for the small, unsuspecting things—things that were birthed directly from my struggles. It's easy to be grateful when life is going well. But what about when life is tough? When life hurts? That's when we need a fresh perspective—to look at things from a different angle. I became an expert in mindful gratitude!

Each day I intentionally looked for the "benefits" of my pain. Anytime I was physically able, I wrote of the blessings I saw when I looked deeply enough to notice. And the blessings were there. Pain really does birth some beautiful things that don't grow in other circumstances.

Because I was looking for blessings, I began noticing great value in things that might seem insignificant at first glance. I focused on my gratitude for the thoughtfulness of a couple of sweet women from my church who set up a box at the end of my hospital bed. Inside that box were scores of small, wrapped packages—one for each day of my journey. They came once a month to replenish my treats, knowing that my love language was gifts. I thanked God daily for their thoughtfulness!

I focused on the blessing of the special cushion brought in for my bed. It was truly fabulous and prevented me from having even one bedsore. And, though I couldn't always eat, I didn't have to prepare myself a meal for nearly ninety days! I didn't do even one load of laundry for months! Despite having to spend Thanksgiving, Christmas, New Year's, and Valentine's Day stuck in a bed in a tiny, drab hospital room, I focused on the blessing of not having to do any shopping or decorating for the holidays. I learned to love the little Christmas tree my mother-in-law set up in my room, and I focused more on the meanings of the holidays than on their traditions. When you are struggling, mindful gratitude may be hard to muster, but it can change your outlook.

I also began to see what my husband was really made of, and I was grateful for the man I saw. Each evening that I was able, we played a game or watched a show together on television. He moved a few necessities in, slept in a recliner beside me for all but one night of the journey, and commuted to his out-of-town job each day. As a direct result of this unwelcomed trial, our marriage was strengthened in gigantic ways. I continue to be so grateful for that blessing, one that was birthed as a direct result of my suffering.

My altered perspective regarding my uninvited trial gave me refreshing clarity that fueled healthy thoughts. Had I not embraced such a perspective, destructive thoughts undoubtedly would have taken over, which would have eventually led to depression, negatively impacting my physical condition. Thankfully, that did not happen, and my healthy thoughts built resilience instead.

Because of my healthy thoughts, I also began to notice a closeness of the Holy Spirit that I had never before experienced. I cannot put into words the peace of that intimacy, the awareness that I wasn't alone. So I embraced it, and I was grateful for it. I began to experience this unwelcomed trial as a sacred, special time, and I didn't want to miss any part of it. I knew I was helpless and that if God chose to bring me through it victoriously, it would forever change the course of my faith in Him and my understanding of His love, mercy, and unmatchable power. I also knew that this spiritual growth would forever change my career as a Christian counselor. I eagerly anticipated getting back to counseling with a fresh dependence on God and the perspective that He *alone* is truly in control. My willingness to view my suffering from this angle would later develop a boldness in my counseling that better equipped me to accomplish what God had called me to do and allowed me to look back on this season of pain with great fondness and thankfulness.

So why is looking at suffering from this unique angle an effective tool? Because it involves gratitude! I admit, when trying to find the good in things that are the result of suffering, we sometimes have to get creative. But this "glass half full, life gives you lemons and you make lemonade" kind of approach can't be beat. Gratitude and discouragement cannot coexist. One will starve out the other. Therefore, if you desire resilience, you must choose to starve the narrow-minded, destructive thoughts that feed your discouragement. You must allow yourself the benefit of viewing your situation from a different angle. And you must even acknowledge some of the blessings that are sometimes subtly hidden within your pain.

In the beginning, you will likely have to force yourself to look at your situation from this angle. This certainly doesn't come naturally. But as I once heard Joni Eareckson Tada say to a group of Christian counselors, "We mouth thanks with hope that it would impact the soul. Thankfulness with the mouth leads to thankfulness in the heart. The spirit catches up and releases depression."[1] Those are wise words from a woman who certainly knows much about long-suffering.

Is Another Perspective Really Enough?

You might be thinking to yourself, *Is this enough? Will embracing mindful gratitude and looking at my suffering from another angle be enough to get me through?* The short answer is no. Why?

Because you must first identify destructive thoughts. And then you must be willing to go to battle.

My colleague Mark, whom I mentioned previously regarding his fight with cancer, has shared with me how he built resilience: "I had to strategically wage war with my head. I preached a sermon to myself daily. Still do!" Truly, much of resilience building is a result of winning a battle of thoughts.

To build resilience, we must clean up repetitive, destructive thoughts about ourselves, about God, about others, and about our situations. Ruminating on such thoughts is like a successful brainwashing, and it powerfully impacts our ability to cope with life's trials. The battleground of the mind is territory for the enemy, and he is rather predictable. So you may find that when you are struggling most, you fixate on thoughts such as:

God isn't helping me.

I can't take another day of this.

Because this happened, I will never be able to experience anything good in life again.

No one understands.

This is awful. I'll never get through this.

I can't handle this.

I am a horrible person.

Consider a day when you struggled intensely. A dark, discouraging day. Now that you have that day in mind, reflect on your thoughts from that time. Undoubtedly, you had some repetitive ones. Powerful thoughts that spiraled you into deeper despair and discouragement. It may help to write down those thoughts, so go ahead and do that, and then consider the following questions: Which thoughts were most discouraging? Most repetitive? Did you have any exaggerations? Catastrophic conclusions? Absolutes? Did you draw conclusions about yourself that you typically don't for other people? Were your thoughts based on your emotions or on the facts? Were you ruminating on false beliefs? Did you have tunnel vision? Were you looking at the situation from only one angle?

You must gain control of destructive thoughts. They are damaging to your mind, emotions, spirit, and body. They impede your choices and your relationships. Most important, they stifle resilience, keep you stuck, and prevent you from bouncing back from life's hurts.

So how do we stop destructive thoughts, which can be extremely fierce, racing forces that seem to take over. How on earth do we stop them? Well, we don't. Not for long anyway. It seems as soon as we manage to stop a destructive thought, it pops up again. Stopping a thought is not enough. We must replace it.

After you've written down a destructive thought, it's time to identify truth. No, not false flattery. Just truth. Notice below how I transformed each of the destructive thoughts we just reviewed into a more accurate truth. You'll notice a form of the familiar "Yes, but . . ." approach we've already discussed in previous chapters.

God is close to the brokenhearted, though sometimes my pain is so intense that I forget His promises.

This is the hardest trial I've ever faced. And I will have to face it day by day. But, with God's help, I will make it.

This has been a tough blow, but I know life has tough seasons. And I have better seasons to look forward to.

Sometimes I feel isolated because my situation seems different from what others are experiencing, but I know everyone faces struggles and pains. Pain is common, though everyone's specific trial is unique to them.

This trial really is challenging. I look forward to when life will not be as sorrowful or difficult.

I can do all things through Christ Who gives me strength.

*I am a child of God, holy and blameless in His sight. Loved
unconditionally by Him. Bought with a price. I have worth
because He is my Creator.*

Repetition and Meditation

Now that we've discovered how to replace destructive thoughts, we
have to get busy with repetition and meditation. Despair results
because we allow our minds to repeat and meditate on destructive thoughts. We play out these negative thoughts in our minds,
giving them our full attention. Therefore, we get ourselves *out* of
despair the same way we got into it: through repetition and meditation. This time we repeat and actively meditate on truth. This
sounds easier than it is. Our destructive thoughts are automatic
and subconscious, which makes them lightning quick. But our
new replacement thoughts are just that—new—which means we
have to consciously think through them. We have to get used to
them. Even while we are trying to replace a negative thought, we
may be pulled right back down by it. Sometimes we have such a
history of thinking destructively that it's as if a weight is attached
to our destructive thoughts and gravity wins!

If this happens to you, as it does to many, then you'll have to
get creative. Write your replacement truths on sticky notes and
make wallpaper out of them. Put them on your mirror in your
bathroom. In your vehicle. At your computer. In your refrigerator.
In your pantry. In your closet. I'm not kidding. Because you are
working against automatic thoughts, you have to be highly intentional in planting seeds of truth. Write a letter to yourself that is
filled with these truths. Write down a list of Scripture verses that
speak truth to your destructive thoughts. Then read these sticky
notes, letters, and verses multiple times a day. Consider this exercise

your prescription to be taken three times a day. Keep replacing. And then keep replacing some more. The repetition of truth has to outweigh the repetition of destructive thoughts before you can begin to bounce back.

Building resilience *requires* replacing false thoughts with truthful ones. When we wage this war, we consciously direct our thinking, and with hard work, we replace our automatic, destructive thoughts with thoughts of hope, truth, gratitude, and sometimes even *mindful* gratitude. Let us echo the words of Psalm 19:14: "May these words of my mouth *and this meditation of my heart* be pleasing in your sight, LORD, my Rock and my Redeemer" (emphasis added). Transforming our thinking is how we bounce back from life's hurts. Notice that we are doing nothing with our circumstances themselves. We are addressing our perspectives and our thoughts *regarding* the circumstances.

Neuroplasticity

At the time that I endured my physical trial, a new aspect of research regarding the brain was just beginning to unfold. Now, as a result of that research, I realize that my healthy thoughts actually changed my brain during that tough season. My thoughts were literally instrumental in determining my physical resilience. Neuroplasticity simply means that the brain is adaptable, for good or bad. The bad news is that the brain can be harmed by toxic thinking. The good news is that the brain can heal as a result of healthy thinking. Significant research in recent years has confirmed that the brain is physiologically impacted by our thinking, and recent advances in brain imaging have made the conclusions of researchers visible for all to see. Dr. Caroline Leaf reports just a few of these fascinating findings in her book *Switch on Your Brain*.[2] She writes about the changes in the structure of our DNA in response to our thoughts, suggesting we have the capacity to do microsurgery on our brains by submitting our thinking to the Holy Spirit. Submitting our thinking to God rewires our thoughts and our choices, and even our brains, and renews our minds. Romans 12:2 has never been more relevant: "Let God transform you into a new person by changing the way you think" (NLT). Our brains are transformed when we, who know God and have access to the wisdom of God through the Holy Spirit, fully embrace the mind of Christ. "But we have the mind of Christ" (1 Cor. 2:16). Yes, we have the mind of Christ! So let's allow Christ to do a full reconstruction of our minds. Let's agree with Him rather than continue to hold on to destructive thoughts that are contrary to His Word. If we are to build resilience and bounce back from the struggles of life, we must take this battle of the mind seriously. We must starve false beliefs. We must repetitiously embrace truth. We must allow ourselves to see our situations from a different angle and to engage in mindful gratitude by seeking out the subtle blessings within our trials. These actions literally change the pathways in our brains and result in measurable changes in our emotional stability, which gets us unstuck from our suffering. A transformed brain is a transformed life!

In a Honduran Hut

Several of us from my church have had the honor over the years to visit some of the remote, primitive villages in Honduras. On a recent visit, I was struck by our interactions with a young couple with several children. As a result of the father's decision to follow Christ, he was disowned by his parents, which meant that he and his family were displaced from the extended family home. A local pastor arranged for him to utilize a small area of land for a home. This father is a hard worker and toiled to build his family a modest hut. Our team had the privilege of helping install in the hut a primitive stove for cooking. My heart sank as we entered the home and took in the scene. The family had nothing. Their newborn baby slept on a repurposed piece of stained and worn padding that was placed on a dirt floor. An old torn towel served as her blanket. They had few material possessions. But when we installed that stove, I witnessed gratitude that couldn't be stifled. They showed pure joy and excitement. I was standing in the same hut, looking at the same situation, but my emotional experience was entirely different from this father's. I felt sorry for him. He felt grateful. I saw what he was missing. He saw what he had gained. I viewed the hut from the angle of my experiences. He viewed it from his. This man taught me about resilience that day. He demonstrated mindful gratitude that I hope to never forget. He bounced back from his pain, not because his situation improved but because his thinking was healthy. He easily could have been stuck in discouragement and unforgiveness. But he was not. He was—and still is—resilient!

Suffering Redefined

My Honduran friend taught me that our suffering needs to be redefined. Not once did he refer to his situation as suffering. As my pastor friend Robert says, "I have observed that those who legitimately suffer, and cope well, *rarely* define their suffering the way we define their suffering." So how would you define your suffering today? Horrible? Endless? Purposeless? It's time to redefine your suffering. Whatever trial you face today, it is a trial with a purpose. And your pains are growing pains. You must learn to look with anticipation for fruit. For blessings. For areas of gratitude. For victories. I train my clients to do this by opening each and every session asking for a list of victories since the last session. I realize that when we are struggling, those victories might seem few and far between, but looking for them and acknowledging them change our perspectives and our thinking about our struggles. Acknowledging the victories God has brought about paves the way for our praise of Him and redefines our suffering. And, friends, *suffering redefined is suffering well!*

Victory Verse

Let the peace that comes from Christ rule in your hearts. . . . And always be thankful. . . . Sing songs and hymns and spiritual songs to God with thankful hearts. And whatever you do or say, do it as a representative of the Lord Jesus, giving thanks through him to God the Father.

Colossians 3:15–17 NLT

Application Questions

1. Mindful gratitude involves looking for the subtle fruits that grow as a direct result of a painful trial. Remember, sometimes we have to get rather creative to demonstrate mindful gratitude, but it is an important aspect of resilience. What are you grateful for in relation to your specific circumstances?

2. One of the easiest ways to see your situation from a different angle is to pretend it is actually not your situation that you are considering. Let's imagine that Sally Jo lives in another state and happens to be in a situation that is a mirror image to yours. You are an observer, as if you are looking through

her window, taking it all in. When you consider the situation from the angle of an observer, what do you see? What do you notice that has been hidden up to this point?

3. As an observer, what do you find yourself wanting to say to encourage Sally Jo?

4. What destructive thoughts were you able to identify after reading this chapter? In what ways have you had tunnel vision regarding your struggles? What has been the effect of these destructive thoughts?

5. Now write down truthful statements and Scripture verses to counteract your destructive thoughts. Place these in numerous areas as an aid in practicing healthy repetition and meditation. Read them multiple times each day, and then enjoy the transformation that takes place as you allow God to renew your mind.

6. What victories have you experienced this week? List them below.

Balance Emotional Boundaries

Madison was eighteen years old and life was going great. He was a star football player and a popular kid with a bright future ahead of him. Admired by many, Madison was finishing his senior year of high school and had recently been nominated by a US congressman to attend the Naval Academy. He also had a full scholarship offer to attend North Carolina State University. The week prior to spring break, Madison began to fast, praying that God would reveal His will for his life: whether he was to attend the Naval Academy, NC State, or do something else. Madison says, "I had been asking repetitively. I had been waiting for an answer. I just wanted God's will in my life."

Madison enjoyed a wonderful time with friends over spring break, exploring Disney and taking in the Florida beaches. On the car ride back from spring break vacation, Madison experienced a life-altering event. With his friend in the driver's seat, Madison propped his legs onto the dash and decided to take a nap. Though Madison has no recollection of the events that followed, he has been told that his friend fell asleep at the wheel and veered off the interstate at full speed and into a concrete road barrier. Their SUV became engulfed in flames on impact. His friend was able to get out of the vehicle and then broke the passenger side window to pull Madison from the flames just in time. Madison was airlifted to a trauma hospital in Florida with a long list of extensive injuries. His T12 vertebra was broken, doctors had to remove a kidney, his pelvis was broken in two places, his right ankle was crushed, and his left ankle was severely burned. His internal organs were displaced by the seat belt, which pushed through his diaphragm, collapsing both of his lungs. His appendix also had to be removed to make room for his stomach, as all his internal organs were swollen.

Madison's parents received the phone call that parents hope and pray never to receive. The hospital gave them the news that Madison was entering emergency surgery that he might not survive. As Madison's parents traveled to be with their son, they made the decision never to ask why in regard to the accident. This turned out to be a profoundly healthy decision that enabled them to cope with the devastation of this event.

Madison underwent numerous surgeries and fought to survive the next couple of months in the hospital, followed by many more months in rehab. Still, today, his suffering continues, as he faces additional surgeries and rehab resulting from further complications. Madison remains paralyzed from the waist down and has had some inevitable times of discouragement. But, ultimately, his hope has never been paralyzed. He holds to the truth of Philippians 3:13–14: "Forgetting what is behind and straining toward what is ahead, I press on toward the goal to win the prize for which God has called me heavenward in Christ Jesus." Madison hopes to walk again one day, but he will likely never play football again. He shares his miracle of life with others on any platform available to him, seeking to integrate this unexpected suffering into God's plan for his life. He would never tell you he likes what has happened to him, but he would tell you that God is using it for good. He hopes to be a congressman one day and keeps his eyes focused on the future as he manages the struggles of today.

The Danger in Overidentifying

With such overwhelming disappointment, so many daily challenges, and so much physical pain, how is Madison living well in his suffering? The same way that he lived well *prior to* his suffering. Prior to the accident, Madison didn't overly identify with his academic success, his athletic abilities, or his popularity. Instead, he prioritized them appropriately. What if Madison had allowed his achievements, good looks, and admiration from others to over-inflate his ego? What if his identity had been heavily grounded in his physical strength and abilities? What if his identity had been strictly rooted in football? If he had overidentified with those things *prior* to the accident, he would not have been nearly as resilient in the *aftermath* of his tragedy. Even wonderful blessings in life can be disastrous to us if we overidentify with them or depend on them for our sense of security and significance.

Madison had a strong foundation prior to his accident, which supported him through the enormous challenges he would face afterward. Consistent with his identity prior to the accident, Madison does not overidentify with his paralysis. It's not that he is in denial either. He deals with the ramifications of that accident every day of his life. It's just that his physical challenges are not the most important thing in his life, no more than his physical prowess was most important prior to the accident. He primarily identifies himself as a child of God; everything else is secondary. And that unchanging identity will carry him through this painful trial as well as any future struggle—or success—in life.

Boundaries

When we think of the word *boundaries*, we often think of toxic people and our need to protect ourselves from them. But, in this case, we're considering the fact that we can be toxic to ourselves and that we need emotional boundaries for ourselves to avoid overidentifying with a traumatic life event, loss, or disappointment.

I'm reminded of the armor listed by Paul in Ephesians 6:13–17 in regard to preparation for battle. Specifically, I consider the importance of the "helmet of salvation" (v. 17). A helmet is designed to protect the head from injury. Any potential threat bounces off the helmet, leaving the head untouched. Why the "helmet of *salvation*"? Because our identity in Christ is most threatened when we suffer a trial, and our hope of salvation is the protection needed for our minds. The enemy incites us to connect our identity with our temporal struggles as opposed to our eternal hope.

Friends, *your helmet of salvation is that much-needed emotional boundary* that protects you from overidentifying with your trial. It is a fence that protects you from dangerously identifying with your suffering. So with your emotional boundary in place, you must ask yourself some important questions regarding your struggles: Is my pain who I am? Or is it something I experience? Does my suffering define me? Or do I define my suffering? Who does my suffering say I am? Who does my God say I am?

Our True Identity

If you overidentify with your trial, then you have some destructive thoughts, specifically about yourself, that are keeping you stuck in your suffering. We've talked at length about destructive thoughts, but here our focus is on your identity. When you are most discouraged, how do you describe yourself?

I am a rape victim.

I am a heart patient.

I am a mother who has lost her child.

I am an orphan.

I am a quadriplegic.

I am a widow.

I am bankrupt.

I am mentally ill.

These descriptions may be true of you, but their placement in the hierarchy of your identity is the key. If you overidentify with your pain, then your suffering is too far up the totem pole of who you are. This exaggerated connection hijacks your identity and may also sabotage your resilience.

So you may be wondering, *Who does God say I am?* According to the Scriptures, if you have trusted in Christ as Lord, then God has a tremendous amount to say about your identity. Consider these truths, as related to your destructive "I ams."

I am His child. (John 1:12)

I am a friend of Jesus. (John 15:5)

I am forgiven, justified, and redeemed. (Rom. 3:24)

I am not condemned. (Rom. 8:1)

I am a fellow heir with Christ. (Rom. 8:17)

I am accepted by Christ. (Rom. 15:7)

I am sanctified. (1 Cor. 1:2)

I am the temple of the Holy Spirit. (1 Cor. 6:19)

I am a new creature in Christ. (2 Cor. 5:17)

I am set free in Christ. (Gal. 5:1)

I am chosen. (Eph. 1:4)

I am holy and blameless in His sight. (Eph. 1:4)

I am adopted into His family. (Eph. 1:5)
I am alive with Christ. (Eph. 2:4–5)
I am His masterpiece, His workmanship. (Eph. 2:10)
I am brought near to God and bought with a price. (Eph. 2:13)
I am cared for. (Phil. 4:19)
I am complete in Christ. (Col. 2:10)

Don't just skim over this list of "I ams." Meditate on them. Read them slowly and repetitively. Dwell on them. Take a look at the Scripture references. Study. Don't move on to the rest of this chapter until you have spent some time absorbing these truths. (Note: this list is only the tip of the iceberg. God has much more to say about who you are. This is just enough to get you thinking. Keep studying His Word to learn even more.)

Imagine God speaking these truths about your identity deep into the well of your being. Imagine these truths transforming your mind. Impacting how you think about yourself. Trumping any misplaced importance you've placed on your suffering.

These truths are your identity! This is who God says you are. This is who you are in sickness and in health, for richer or poorer. These are solid, unshakable facts about you that cannot be swayed by circumstance, good or bad. Your suffering is an *experience*. This is your *identity*!

Do you notice the difference between these two lists of "I ams"? The first list leads to emptiness. The second list leads to hope. It is vitally important that you acknowledge the facts that may be present on the first list but identify yourself according to the second list.

Trials, traumas, and losses are significant; they are painful. If you've experienced horrific hurt, then you feel it to your core. Your life won't be the same again. To protect your identity, you must compartmentalize your painful trial as an experience, but not an experience that defines you. If your painful trial involves the loss of someone you love, it may be particularly challenging to protect your identity. You may think, *Because I really loved them, I cannot compartmentalize my pain. They deserve more honor than that.* Again, you are not going to deny the truth about your painful trial or even the significance of someone you have lost. But you are going to focus on a healthy identity; one that is built on the foundation of God's truths.

Imagine the impact of fully embracing your *true* identity: who God defines you as being. How freeing! How hope-giving! How life-changing!

So when you have a thought about yourself that is inconsistent with who God says you are, imagine that thought bouncing off you like a pebble off a helmet. Think of that helmet as the emotional boundary of your mind, keeping out anything other than your identity in Christ. No trial, no struggle, no rejection, no trauma, no loss, no disappointment, no suffering defines you. The only thoughts that pass through your helmet are those that reflect *who God says you are.* His is the only opinion that matters, and His opinion absolutely carries more weight than your circumstance.

I'll remind you that repetition of truth is a requirement for resilience. If you have wrestled with your identity, then meditating on these truths about who you are is crucial. You will need to invest significant concentration, time, and attention in challenging destructive thoughts about yourself. We've already discussed the neurological impact of shifting from negative ruminations to truth. Those same principles apply to the transformation of your identity.

LeeAnn

LeeAnn is a delightful young woman. She will tell you that it is not she who is delightful but Christ in her. She is quick to share

117

her faith, and her enthusiasm about her relationship with God is genuine and contagious. Despite having experienced many losses, she has a refreshing countenance and attitude. With each of her pregnancies—and there have been four—she celebrated the miraculous gift of life. But, unfortunately, LeeAnn lost each of those four children due to miscarriages. She has been riding a chronic emotional roller coaster of incredible joy and hope, followed by deep and intense sadness. Her unpredictable journey has caused suffering that could shake the emotional stability of even the healthiest individuals.

Many who face a similar trial identify themselves by their brokenness.

I am inadequate as a female.
I have a broken body.
I am barren.
Who am I, if not a mother?

Despite the very real vulnerability, LeeAnn has never dwelled on any of these thoughts. And despite intense grief, she isn't emotionally unstable.

Identity Crisis

How has LeeAnn avoided emotional instability, though she has experienced tremendous situational instability? She has never experienced an identity crisis. You see, trials may invite an identity crisis because we often don't have a healthy foundation prior to the onset of our suffering. We're often overly enmeshed in the things that are going our way before the onset of a trial (success, relationships, physical health or appearance), and therefore we are also mistakenly overly connected to the inevitable struggles of life (loss, suffering, rejection, physical decline). *Emotional instability always results from a false identity.* When our identity is too connected to our circumstances, our sense of self fluctuates as does our emotional well-being. When our identity is excessively attached to our hurts, we prolong our suffering and invite additional, unnecessary pain. We become stuck, and resilience appears out of reach.

Identity Theft

The government, banks, and various companies often warn of the implications of the crime of identity theft and caution us to take specific steps that will protect us from it. When someone is the victim of a dishonest person stealing their identity, it results in financial distress and an incredible sense of vulnerability. It also sometimes takes hundreds of hours to correct the damage. But what about identity theft at the hands of despair? Or because we inappropriately connect our struggles to our personal worth? We must guard against this serious threat, and we must be consciously aware of our vulnerability.

Identity Protection

In contrast, can you imagine for a moment what happens when our identity is primarily connected to our faith in Christ? We experience greater stability—and resilience! Don't get me wrong. It is not a perfect stability. Trials are sometimes incredibly intense, so they may shake us for a time. We are also living imperfect lives, with imperfect minds, in an imperfect world, with imperfect circumstances. Therefore, our sense of self will never be perfectly whole this side of eternity. But we have hope for a resilient identity. And that requires identity protection provided through healthy and balanced emotional boundaries. "He must become greater; I must become less" (John 3:30). Less of me. Less of my suffering. More of Christ. We must apply the appropriate weight to our struggles—and also to Christ. This means allowing the pendulum to swing, as it has been overly weighted with our trials and pains. Only when the pendulum swings do we experience resilience. This is the making of a stable sense of self.

The significant ingredient here is Christ, who never changes. "Jesus Christ is the same yesterday and today and forever" (Heb. 13:8). If we want stability, it makes sense to draw close to a source of stability, and Christ is the Rock. Nothing shakes Him. Nothing changes His identity. Nothing creates a crisis for Him. Though He has suffered and grieved, He remains unmoved. We need no boundary with Him. We are to remain in Him, and He in us (see John 15:4). The more we abide in Christ and allow him into our lives and into our suffering, the more stable our identity becomes. This is an everlasting solution to an unnecessary identity crisis following unwelcomed suffering.

Though their extremely challenging circumstances have not improved, Madison and LeeAnn both remain stable and hopeful. And it is certainly not because they've been sheltered from pain. They live in this hostile world, just as you and I do. They too have experienced unpredictable and harsh circumstances. LeeAnn's losses have been repetitive and long-enduring. Madison's losses continue to be life-altering in every way imaginable. But they are both resilient because their identities in Christ have had more power in their lives than their suffering. In fact, I know these two individuals have healthy identities because I see more Christ than suffering in them. They are living well in their pain. And so it is with you, and with me. Our identities cannot rest on our circumstances any more than it can rest on our job or school performance, our popularity, or our physical appearance. Self-identity must rest on a permanent foundation—Christ—a foundation that cannot be destroyed by the inevitable storms of life.

Is It Possible to Inadvertently Worship Our Suffering?

"I am the first and I am the last; apart from me there is no God. . . . Is there any God besides me? No, there is no other Rock; I know not one" (Isa. 44:6, 8). Though our intention certainly is never to worship our suffering, when it becomes too significant in forming our identity, it has indeed become a form of idolatry, a focus of our attention that has been awarded too much weight. Let's ask ourselves, Who, or what, created me? Who, or what, shapes my future? Who, or what, is the object of my time and attention? Who, or what, defines me? Yes, certainly on occasion a normal season of suffering gains your full attention and temporarily monopolizes your life. If your pain has just recently entered your life, then this discussion is not for you. But when a season of loss becomes a permanent powerhouse, a twisted form of idolatry has likely snuck its way in. As if the hurt wasn't challenging enough in and of itself, the enemy then uses it against you even more as it is awarded an inappropriate level of power to shape your sense of self and define your future.

If this type of imbalance describes you, then don't wait until tomorrow. Unaddressed idolatry never ends well. Determining your own God profits you nothing (see Isa. 44:10). So simply confess this realization to God now. Affirm His lordship in your life and begin your work to correct the inappropriate balance. Remind yourself, and your enemy, of your commitment to God. God reveals truth out of His great love for you. He knows you never meant to make suffering an idol, and He holds no condemnation. He desires to rescue your false identity and free you to become who He has created you to be. So make the choice not to camp out in this imbalance any longer. Your suffering will no longer define you or corrupt your self-worth; turn from its lingering manipulation.

But What if I Made This Mess I Am In?

This chapter may be tough for you to read if your pain is the result of some of your mistakes and if your identity has been inadvertently altered by those previous choices. You may beat yourself up routinely, feeling that you are unworthy because of some of the decisions you have made. You've created a mess; therefore, you think of yourself as a mess. I'm reminded of the woman at the well with Jesus described in John 4. He was a Jew; she was a Samaritan. This was unusual because Jews didn't associate with Samaritans. It was a boundary. And Jesus crossed a line in asking her for a drink. Then his conversation with her uncovered the poor choices she had made. No sense denying them. But He also revealed to her the rest of the story: He is Living Water and she never needed to thirst again (see John 4:13). He was her solution. He broke the rules, and in doing so, He also broke through her identity crisis. He crossed a boundary that had been wrongly placed. He spoke truth about who she was. And, more important, who *He* was. She believed Him, left her water jar right where it was, and immediately began testifying to others about the truth. If you are struggling today, tormented by your previous choices, let Him do the same for you. Believe what He says about you. And what He says about Himself. His Living Water applies to you, just as it did the Samaritan woman.

A Beautiful Balance

Maybe you just feel unworthy because of the struggles your storm has automatically swept into your life. Struggles you can't ignore— or get away from. After reading this chapter, you realize you have overidentified with your pain. You have allowed it to define you.

Let's take a glance at Moses to see how he bounced back from an uninvited false identity. You see, Moses, as a result of a series of circumstances that he neither earned nor controlled, found himself in the family of his enemy. He was one of them. Adopted into a lineage he didn't desire. So how did he respond? "By faith Moses, when he had grown up, refused to be known as the son of Pharaoh's daughter" (Heb. 11:24). Moses rejected a false identity and instead embraced his true identity. His history was secondary. Moses knew who he really was. Despite any hardship. Any challenges. He made a conscious choice to place a healthy emotional boundary around his sense of self. One that protected him from a past he rejected.

If you are inspired by Moses's bold refusal, then today is your day. This is the day that you begin defining your suffering rather than allowing your suffering to define you. With God's help and direction, you determine the value of your pain. You determine the weight of its power in shaping your sense of significance. Today is the day you reprioritize God's truths about you. Now is the time for some serious redefining!

Those who cope best neither deny nor overidentify with their pain. They don't disassociate from their suffering, and they don't exaggerate the importance of their suffering. They have a beautiful balance in boundaries, even in ugly circumstances. I pray that you have that balance or you are in the process of finding it and that you will continue to hold fast to your *true* identity. Yours will be a stable, unchanging, abiding faith in Christ that will allow you to bounce back from life's toughest blows.

Victory Verse

He must become greater; I must become less.

John 3:30

Application Questions

1. You learned in this chapter that it's important to establish healthy emotional boundaries in your suffering and to compartmentalize your painful trial as an experience rather than an identity. Is this a transition you need to make? What difference might it make in your life if you do?

2. Consider some of your most challenging days when you have been most overwhelmed and discouraged by your circumstances. What are your destructive "I ams"? Write them down below.

   What do you notice about your personal list of "I ams"? How has your pain defined you? *Remember, you may identify yourself by some descriptors that may be true of you, but they may be misplaced in the hierarchy of your identity. If you overidentify with your pain, then your suffering is too far up the totem pole of who you are. This exaggerated connection between your suffering and your identity may be keeping you stuck.*

3. Look over the list of healthy "I ams" earlier in this chapter. Which truths are most difficult for you to accept for yourself? Which truths do you most need to be reminded of? *Please understand that these scriptural truths really do apply to you if you are a child of God, whether or not you feel they do. God's truths trump any messages from your pain. It is critical that you make a choice to agree with God about who you are. Remember, anytime you reject something God has stated, you are committing sin. Rejecting the value He has placed on you is sinful because you are disagreeing with Him. It really is that simple. Agreeing with God about who you are in Him—regardless of your circumstances—frees you from being stuck and lays a*

foundation for resilience because it is a basic act of obedience to Him.

Imagine living your life with this healthy identity as your backdrop. Imagine these truths being your automatic thoughts regarding yourself. What would this be like? How might this healthy backdrop impact your ability to bounce back from the specific struggles you currently face?

4. We've discussed in this chapter the importance of shifting the pendulum: "He must become greater; I must become less" (John 3:30). Less of me (and my struggle), more of Christ (and how He defines me). How does this speak to your heart and your situation today?

Maintain Healthy Relationships

In May 2015, Solene received word of her sister's disappearance. Mary, an early dementia patient, had wandered from her home. Her disappearance was immediately followed by an intense search by Lake City, Florida, law enforcement as well as many family members and friends. Minutes turned to hours, which turned to days. Days turned into weeks, and then months. There was no indication of Mary's whereabouts. No clues. No encouragement. And still today, as I write this chapter, more than a year since her disappearance, there is no evidence of where Mary might be.

Can you imagine? The sister you grew up with, shared secrets with, shared bedrooms with, shared memories with . . . suddenly vanished. No one can find her. What has happened to her? Has she been taken? Is she alive? Is she cold? Has she eaten? Does she understand what's happening? Has someone harmed her? Is she dead?

How do we cope when we have no resolution? Oftentimes, the unknowns are the hardest to handle. We may be most shaken when a disturbing mystery is linked to our suffering. And so it is with Solene.

A few months ago, I was at a local women's event. I selected a specific table to join for dinner because I noticed Solene sitting at it, and I wanted to inquire as to the progress in the search for Mary. I learned that there had been no progress. Being the inquisitive counselor type, I continued to probe. "How are you managing this? You are here at this event. I see you at other events. How are you doing this?" I asked her.

In her matter-of-fact style, Solene confirmed that she was suffering greatly as a result of this tragedy, oftentimes getting stuck in what-ifs or contemplating the various catastrophic events that could have possibly led to Mary's disappearance. But she also confirmed that staying connected to the body of Christ was an intentional choice because she knew it was a necessary aspect to her survival. "I decided right away that I had to be in church. And, specifically, I had to stay in the choir. I needed to be there. I needed the routine, and I needed that family of people," she said. When isolation might have felt as if it were the most welcoming option, Solene chose a harder but healthier route, and that choice has been both a result of and a catalyst for her resilience.

Hopefully, today you are not grieving the mysterious loss of a sibling. But you are probably facing something challenging or you wouldn't be reading this book. Because pain often creates isolation, you may be tempted to face this journey alone. The truth is that when we are suffering, more energy than normal is required of us to be around other people, even those we love and have previously enjoyed socializing with. We don't want to fake a smile. And we don't have the patience for some of the trivial conversations that sometimes arise in everyday relationships. When intensely struggling, we may only be able to be with a few people. We may be in a season in which we have little to offer back. It's good to be reminded that the intensity of our season will change, and we need those relationships to remain intact so that it will be easier to get more involved when we are better able to do so. Making the choice to routinely and intentionally connect with our support systems is a significant aspect of resilience. Continuing to live life with friends and family is a necessary ingredient to bouncing back from life's hurts.

How Do I Connect?

If connecting with friends and family on a deep level is a challenge, then it's time to get creative.

Support Groups

Seek out support groups connected with your local church. Many churches now offer groups for those who are grieving or experiencing depression, cancer, a chronic illness, an addiction, an eating disorder, or a divorce. Many churches also offer support groups for those who have been left behind following the suicide of a loved one or those who are weary caregivers of dementia patients. The options are endless. Ask your pastor, your physician, or a counselor for information regarding local resources. Support groups are powerfully effective, so much so that they are sometimes more helpful than individual counseling simply because of the connections and relationships with others who are experiencing similar difficulties. We, indeed, are designed to live life in community. We are created to carry one another's burdens, to be a "neighbor" to others, and to allow others to do likewise.

Social Media

As a counselor who has seen a lot of destruction at the hands of social media, I must admit that I am reluctant to recommend this venue for connecting with others. However, it can be effective when used appropriately and when other methods of connecting are limited. Remember Mark, my colleague who fought leukemia and, later, male breast cancer? Here are some of his thoughts on the use of social media.

I can remember a snow day several years ago when I created my Facebook profile. Little did I know what that investment would return to me many years later. Before social media, in 1991, I went to Seattle, Washington, for a bone marrow transplant. I spent forty-five days in a bubble, in total isolation, in order to prepare my body to receive the transplant. It was in that isolation that Jesus taught me that He was enough: Jesus plus nothing. Jesus minus nothing.

I spent the next twenty years with that mind-set: it was me and Jesus. I ministered to others, and I did not set myself up to do life completely and authentically with others. My breast cancer diagnosis came on the trip to Africa. I can remember making a conscious decision that I did not want to go through this secretly. That I needed other people. So, sitting in an internet café in a little village in Africa, I posted my diagnosis to Facebook. Immediately, the power went out. Two days later, we had internet access again. I checked my Facebook page and was overwhelmed by the prayers, kind words, and encouragement. This interaction continued throughout my cancer protocol of chemo and radiation. Those Facebook posts, messages, and helpful links were like medicine to my soul. My first cancer experience taught me that Jesus was enough. My second experience taught me that He works through people and that I need to be connected to them. Almost daily, someone would send me a song, a Scripture, or just a personal word that God used in an incredible way in my life.

Technological advances have awarded us unusual opportunities to remain connected with our loved ones. So when your circumstances prevent you from being able to fully address your isolation, it's time to get creative. Tune in to church services via TV or live stream on the internet. Prayerfully consider the possibility of remaining linked with the body of Christ through social media. With appropriate boundaries in place, this can be a wonderful venue and may assist in preventing you from becoming stuck.

Caution: When to Connect and Disconnect

When we are in the midst of a challenging storm, we benefit from staying connected to the right people. And sometimes we need to disconnect from toxic people. Obviously, this is a time when we need discernment. Amid a struggle, our connections need to be primarily with people who are emotionally and spiritually healthy, who are actively involved in the body of Christ, who encourage us, who are growing in their relationships with God, and who have other healthy relationships as well. These people don't draw near to us in our suffering out of curiosity or for purposes of gossip. These people can be trusted. These are people who are compassionate but not enabling, who are not afraid to challenge us with the truth when we need it, who are resilient. And resilience is contagious! So let's allow a few resilient people to rub off on us by keeping them in our inner circles.

Unfortunately, resilience is not the only contagious response to struggle. You've heard the phrase "Misery loves company." It's true, and that's why some connections will not be helpful in times of intense pain. In fact, these connections may be quite dangerous. When suffering, we don't have the same level of tolerance for difficult people in our lives. We're not on our "game," so to speak. We need to make sure we have appropriate boundaries with those who are content being stuck and would prefer if we did the same.

Job is known for the terrible suffering he endured because of a spiritual battle that had nothing to do with him. God Himself identified Job as a righteous man, a "servant . . . blameless and upright"

(Job 1:8). Satan wanted to prove that Job was just a shallow follower and if he were to suffer, he'd curse God. So the onslaught began. Unfortunately, Job also had a few sidekicks, some toxic friends who gave a host of inaccurate explanations for Job's suffering. They added fuel to his pain, and the enemy used them to add further turmoil and confusion to Job's life. These friends didn't necessarily mean to be toxic. But they were, because they were without true knowledge. Satan lost the victory he was hoping for, and eventually, Satan and Job's friends were silenced. But God was not.

The lesson for us? While it's vitally important to remain connected to others, we must be careful about whom we allow to counsel us. If we connect to toxic people and allow them too much influence over our struggles, their presence will only add to our suffering.

Caution: A Word about Comparisons

Anytime we connect with others, it invites the possibility of an unhealthy comparison. And this is particularly true when we are struggling. Yes, we still need to live life with other people. But we must guard our hearts and minds against the temptation to compare our complicated lives to what appears to be the perfect lives of those around us. Of course, no one lives a completely easy and pain-free life, but when we look at the lives of others with an unhealthy filter, we may make some incorrect assumptions. Comparison can create envy, discontent, pity, and despair. So as you connect, be careful about the enemy's desire to use the relationship to keep you stuck, asking yourself, "Why me?" Remember, "Why?" might be the most common question we ask, but it's not the healthiest. A replacement might be, "Why *not* me? Everyone struggles with something." Comparisons cause disappointment because we develop a "grass is greener syndrome" and falsely assume that other people experience no struggle. That is never true, and it is the very reason that reaching out to help others helps us in our suffering. It reminds us of the struggle that is part of every human being's existence and our need for hope and encouragement this side of eternity. This is a necessary shift in perspective that aids in building resilience.

If you find yourself comparing yourself to others, then take a personal time-out and tell yourself the whole story. Yes, you are struggling. And so are they. Their struggle may not presently be as intense as yours, but I promise you they have a story. Everyone does. Take the time to notice their story and temporarily take your eyes off your own. This is likely the remedy to the additional struggle brought on by your temptation to compare.

The Body of Christ

Our culture has changed immensely. Years ago, our ancestors lived in community, with extended families often living in the same home together, and communities working together to meet one another's needs. Now we live lives of isolation. We are independent to a fault. We hardly know how to connect. We need a refresher in an Old Testament truth:

> Two are better than one, because they have a good return for their labor: If either of them falls down, one can help the other up. But pity anyone who falls and has no one to help them up. Also, if two lie down together, they will keep warm. But how can one keep warm alone? Though one may be overpowered, two can defend themselves. A cord of three strands is not quickly broken. (Eccles. 4:9–12)

Consider the remote villages in Honduras where poverty-stricken families build huts encircling a large soccer field. They've designed their entire villages around their need to live life in community, with numerous strands forming a strong cord. They've discovered something that we seem to have forgotten.

> But God has put the body together . . . so that there should be no division in the body, but that its parts should have equal concern for each other. If one part suffers, every part suffers with it; if one part is honored, every part rejoices with it. (1 Cor. 12:24–26)

It is God's plan that we as Christians live life with one another—both when life is good and when times are tough. We aren't to be isolated individuals, concerned only for ourselves, but "members of [God's] household" (Eph. 2:19). Therefore, at times we must be the givers of compassion and altruism, and at times we must be the recipients. Though our roles may change, the body of Christ is to be a constant source of connection, with consistency unaffected by circumstances. "In Christ we, though many, form one body, and each member belongs to all the others" (Rom. 12:5). It is not only God's design but also His command. He specifically instructs us to stay joined to the body of Christ. And since He is the Master Designer, He knows best what is good for us and what is good for His body.

Connection within the Body of Christ

Pain doesn't just isolate. It causes us to turn inward. Pain invites tunnel vision and an unintentional (and unhealthy) focus on self. When we are *stuck* in suffering, we become destructively absorbed in our thoughts, needs, and pains. We become preoccupied with ourselves. We have a pity party! Let's be clear: we don't *intend* to be self-centered or self-absorbed. It's just that this inward focus is a natural, almost instinctual, consequence of suffering. When we struggle, it becomes difficult for us to see outside ourselves. This is precisely why staying connected with others builds resilience. As my friend Mark says, "Pity is like junk food—it will not sustain you!" With that said, it's important to connect not only with others but also with the *needs* of others. This link broadens our focus, turns us outward rather than inward, and is the perfect solution to self-absorbed tunnel vision.

In chapter 6, I told you about a lengthy hospitalization I was forced to endure a number of years ago. I shared with you that I came to a point where I was able to view my suffering from a different angle. But I also began to realize that, though helpless in a bed and though it seemed my world had come to a halt, I was surrounded by others who were continuing to live life. And I needed to be connected to them. I also realized that, though my body was struggling, my spiritual gifts were still intact. God was simply providing me with a different platform.

I tell people I am the same person whether I am in my office counseling or out to dinner with friends. The same was true during this season in the hospital. I was the same person, and God still desired to use me. I was grateful for that realization, so I responded. I didn't counsel per se, but I did begin looking for ways to encourage my nurses and inquire about their lives. You don't have to look very far to notice that everyone is hurting in some manner. And when you live somewhere for three months, you have tons of time to get to know your caregivers! I recall numerous nights with a couple of those sweet nurses as they sat at the end of my bed and shared their lives with me. We prayed together, they ministered to my physical needs, and I was able to encourage them. Soon my physician began writing orders for a few other patients to be brought into my room for encouragement and coaching about how to manage their physical and emotional challenges. My situation was more critical than the situations of those around me, so much so that I could never leave my room or even my bed. Rather than having a pity party about that fact, I chose to see the value of my situation being more severe than theirs. I was grateful, because it gave me credibility to speak about dealing with difficulty. It heightened the effectiveness of my new platform. My trial brought with it a special opportunity I had never had before, and I enjoyed connecting with others around me in a unique manner, despite my physical struggles.

Whatever your situation, I encourage you to take the time to look outside yourself. What is going on in the lives of those around you? Remember, pity starves you of connections and perspective that builds your resilience. Fight that urge to focus inwardly and build resilience by looking outside yourself and your very familiar pain. Every day look for ways to encourage and pray for others. Don't fence yourself in with your self-pity. Remember, everyone struggles with something. So while you struggle, pray for other people. When you are sad, write a card of encouragement to someone else. When you are discouraged, inquire as to how someone else is doing. Listen to their struggle. Validate them. Pray with and for them. This is good for them—and it will also be very good for you.

Paul

Many examples of connection within the body of Christ can be found in God's Word. For example, let's look at the life of the apostle Paul. Few people in Scripture endured the level of suffering that Paul did. In and out of prisons. Beaten. Flogged. Shipwrecked. Stoned. Criticized and distrusted. Rejected and threatened. Yet resilient! In fact, he is easily one of the most influential individuals in history, writing most of the New Testament and mentoring and inspiring other Christian leaders along the way. And what one characteristic of Paul continued throughout his Christian life? His connectedness to church bodies and to friends of Christ.

Throughout his journeys, Paul made extra effort, even in times of suffering, to connect with others. To update them. To encourage them. To admonish them. To ask for their prayers. He reached out to others and also allowed them to reach out to him. He was both a giver and a recipient in his connection with God's people. He traveled long distances to visit in person when he could and wrote letters when he could not. The following verses from the book of Philippians give us a glimpse into the importance of relationships in Paul's life:

> Every time I think of you, I give thanks to my God. Whenever I pray, I make my requests for all of you with joy, for you have been my partners in spreading the Good News about Christ from the time you first heard it until now. . . . So it is right that I should feel as I do about all of you, for you have a special place in my heart. You share with me the special favor of God, both in my imprisonment and in defending and confirming the truth of the Good News. God knows how much I love you and long for you with the tender compassion of Christ Jesus. (1:3–5, 7–8 NLT)

One of the most profound examples of Paul's connection to others occurred during his imprisonment with Silas (see Acts 16:16–40). After Paul commanded an evil spirit to leave a young girl, the two men were brought to the city, where they were stripped, beaten, and severely flogged. Their feet were fastened in the stocks of an inner cell in the prison. Acts 16:25 reports that at "around midnight Paul and Silas were praying and singing hymns to God." These men stuck together in their suffering. And they stuck to God.

We know from Scripture that a series of events followed their prayers and songs of praise: an earthquake shook the land, the prison doors were opened, and the chains of every prisoner fell off. The jailer, thinking the prisoners had escaped, was prepared to take his own life. Paul and Silas revealed that they were still in their cell and urgently called out to the guard: "Don't harm yourself!" (v. 28). The jailer then fell at their feet, asking what he needed to do to be saved. Indeed, the jailer was saved, along with his entire family, and Paul and Silas were released. And what did they do after they left the prison? They immediately went to Lydia's house, "where they met with the brothers and encouraged them" (v. 40). Whether in suffering or in celebration following respite from struggle, Paul stayed connected to others. Paul was an incredibly resilient man. And I believe that his connection to the body of Christ and his ability to look outward instead of inward fueled his ability to cope with the intense suffering he endured in life.

Lazarus

Many of us are familiar with the story of the death of Lazarus. Lazarus was Jesus's dear friend and had been dead four days before Christ got to him. Jesus was moved by the death of His friend and the raw emotion of many who gathered around Him, including Lazarus's sisters, Mary and Martha. They were suffering. They had lost their friend and brother, and they were disappointed that Jesus hadn't arrived in time to help. When Mary and Martha brought Jesus to the tomb, Jesus said in a loud voice, "Lazarus, come out!" (v. 43). And when this previously dead man came out of the tomb, Jesus instructed, "Take off the grave clothes and let him go" (v. 44). Jesus could have done this without any assistance from the onlookers. Seriously. He had just raised Lazarus from the dead! Certainly He could have miraculously removed the grave clothes with one swift word. Or He could have instructed Lazarus to do this for himself. But He didn't. Jesus specifically instructed that other people actively participate in removing Lazarus's grave clothes. Though Lazarus had undoubtedly been a giver in times previous, on this day it was God's design that he be the recipient of care and compassion. God intended and even orchestrated that Lazarus be with other people during this monumental event in his life.

Likewise, Jesus instructs that we live our lives together with others. We are to "take off the grave clothes" of one another. "Carry each other's burdens, and in this way you will fulfill the law of Christ" (Gal. 6:2). It's an easy command: look for a burden in someone else's life and determine to help bear it. Also, allow them to do the same for you. Maybe today you are a Lazarus. Maybe today you are one of his friends. The bottom line is this: we all have struggles and God's Word instructs us to share the weight of our suffering with one another.

So if your friend is struggling, carry some of that weight. If your spouse is struggling, carry some of that weight. If your children are struggling, carry some of that weight. If *you* are struggling, allow some of your weight to be carried by others. I love the marriage and family model developed by doctors Tom and Beverly Rodgers that encourages spouses and family members to participate with God in the healing of emotional wounds through what they call "Soul Healing Love."[1] By participating in the healing, we address the hurts that could otherwise potentially destroy a marriage and family. Some hurts are bigger than we are. And God often uses other people in our lives to serve as a balm and salve for those hurts.

We Need One Another

Anytime I have a new client in a crisis, I ask a lot of questions. I want to know the full picture. The circumstances of the crisis. The challenges that hinder. I also want to know about their strengths. One particular area I focus on is their social supports. I want to know whether they have adequate support from family and friends. I want to know about their involvement in the local church. I want to know about their work environment. Why? Because the support of others has a powerful effect on resilience. And if no support is present, then we have to find ways to build it.

Researchers are also now discovering the health impacts of social support. "Those with high quality or quantity social networks have a decreased risk of mortality in comparison to those who have low quantity or quality of social relationships. . . . In fact, social isolation itself was identified as an independent major risk factor for all-cause mortality."[2] What does this say to me? First, it confirms that we all will suffer. But isolation may make our suffering more unbearable and may even contribute to a premature death. On the contrary, social support helps us bounce back from life's physical and emotional hurts.

We need one another. Staying connected will protect us from emotional, and even physical, decline and make it easier for us to fully transition back into life when we are ready. But let's not stop with simply being connected. Let's make sure that our outward focus propels us to connect with the *needs* of those around us. Let's look for ways to encourage others and enjoy the medicinal benefits of being healthy, active members of the body of Christ!

Victory Verse

Carry each other's burdens, and in this way you will fulfill the law of Christ.

Galatians 6:2

Application Questions

1. When you face a trial, do you tend to isolate yourself from others? If so, how has behaving this way robbed you?

2. If you don't have a support network, where might you start? (Coffee with a coworker, a phone call to a friend or relative, or lunch with a neighbor may be a simple launching point.)

3. How do you think having an inward focus might impact your resilience?

4. In what ways have you reached out to others amid your suffering? What impact has reaching out had on your coping abilities?

5. When you are stuck in an inward focus, you may not notice the struggles in the lives of those around you. Take a moment to look at people around you. What are their hurts? How does this provide a different perspective on your personal struggle?

Practice Self-Care

Timothy suffered more religious persecution than any other human being I have ever met. A modern-day Paul, Timothy changed his name after narrowly escaping execution in an Egyptian prison. His suffering was at the hands of Muslim radicals who were once his brothers. Timothy had been a radical leader himself, a fundamentalist member of the Muslim Brotherhood. In an attempt to convert a Christian to Islam, Timothy began to study the Bible, only to conclude that Jesus is the Savior. He eventually converted to Christianity and was well aware of the potential consequences of his conversion. When a member of the brotherhood converts, they are given three days to recant. If they do not, then they are killed in the name of Allah. Timothy was secretly baptized in a pastor's home, but when he led another Islamic brother to Christ, his conversion was made public. Following his admission of faith in Christ, Timothy was stoned and beaten by the brotherhood in front of the mosque where he had formerly zealously preached Islam. According to Timothy's brothers, he was a blasphemous infidel who deserved death. They regarded his conversion as the most horrendous form of desecrating Islam and the Qur'an. When it was time for Timothy to recant, outraged Muslims barbarically raided his home. His mother begged them to kill her instead. Soon afterward, she publicly disowned and disinherited Timothy.

Timothy fled and sought refuge with underground Christians, but they feared sheltering him, so he faced this frightening journey alone. He was hunted by Muslims from city to city. "I learned what it means to have God as my only hiding place," he said. Finally, he found short-term shelter in Cairo, Egypt, where he was encouraged and sheltered by a Christian friend. Because his friend was jeopardizing his life and the lives of his family members, Timothy decided to return to his village, where his family reported him. He was arrested and released repeatedly. After his last arrest, he was informed that if he were ever arrested again, he would be charged with high treason and would be executed. However, God showed up and paved the way for Timothy's exit from Egypt. Timothy is now, many years later, a US citizen who works to spread the gospel to the Muslim world.[1]

I met Timothy shortly after he arrived in the United States. I enjoyed occasionally spending time with him and helping him assimilate into a new culture and community. Like others who met him, I was enthralled by his story and blown away by his faith and courage in the face of unbelievable circumstances. I also saw how he continued to live in fear—legitimate fear. He was still considered an enemy of his country, an infidel who caused national disunity, and he lived constantly under the threat of retaliation.

How does a person bounce back from that kind of trauma? How can someone build resilience while living under extreme distress and relentless danger?

When I think about Timothy, I'm reminded that resilience doesn't come easily. When Timothy first came to the United States, he was eager to share his testimony and to give God glory for the unthinkable acts of persecution he had narrowly survived. Then Timothy began to notice a pattern. Whenever he delved excessively into the details of his story, his post-traumatic stress disorder worsened. So in order to continue to do what he felt God had called him to do, he had to adjust how he shared his story. To avoid having nightmares and flashbacks and to remain effective in ministry, he began to provide fewer details about his trauma.

Timothy's experiences have undoubtedly left scars. But because he took some basic steps to protect his mental health, he has prevented his horrible past from leaving gaping wounds that would keep him stuck in his present suffering and render him ineffective for the gospel. Timothy is one of my heroes in the faith. He's also a hero in resilience!

In this chapter, you'll learn some practical self-care strategies, similar to the ones Timothy utilized, designed to facilitate resilience and protect you from the shackles that can keep you stuck in your suffering.

Is Self-Care Biblical?

Now before you start thinking that self-care is some new age strategy or argue that it is inappropriate for a person of faith to look for ways to care for themselves, let's check Scripture. Which biblical example testifies to the importance of self-care? Surely the Bible contains at least one. Yes, it does, and it's found in the story of Elijah in 1 Kings 19.

Elijah, a prophet and man of God, came to a life season in which he became weary and discouraged; he was trying to prophesy to people who wouldn't listen to him and had an enemy breathing down his neck. So what did he do? Was he a model of resilience? Not exactly. When his life was in danger, Elijah, already disappointed, discontent, and despondent, literally ran away and isolated himself (see vv. 1–4). He further complicated a bad situation and became very depressed. His running and isolation didn't help him. In fact, running away and isolating himself worsened his thoughts of being a failure and heightened his fears of his enemy. Finally, he expressed his despair: "I have had enough, LORD. . . . Take my life" (v. 4). He prayed that he would die! (I know some of you can relate to this level of despair.) After Elijah prayed to die, he fell asleep. An angel woke him after some time and said, "Get up and eat" (v. 5). Elijah ate and drank and lay down again to sleep. After resting for some time, Elijah was touched by the angel and instructed once again to "get up and eat" (v. 7),which he did. Strengthened by the food, Elijah traveled forty days and forty nights to Horeb, where he found a cave and slept again. God not only allowed Elijah to sleep but also directed him to eat. Only *after* Elijah's physical needs were addressed did God pose the question that fueled Elijah's resilience: "What are you doing here, Elijah?" (v. 13). God's question served as a reality check.

"What are you doing here?" It's a good question for us to ask ourselves as well. If you are stuck today, address your physical needs first and then ask yourself, "What am I doing here? How did I get here?"

Now that we've established that the Bible addresses the importance of meeting one's basic physical needs—including getting adequate nutrition and rest—let's open our toolbox to see what other tools we might use to best care for ourselves. Listed below are some of the most practical and effective self-care tools you will find for building resilience. So read on, pick out a few tools, and let the building begin!

Laugh

When Teena's youngest daughter, Sylvana, was just an infant, she was diagnosed with biliary atresia, an extremely rare liver disease.

To survive, she would need surgery, many follow-up medical treatments, and eventually a liver transplant. Teena's marriage did not survive long after Sylvana's diagnosis, and Teena was left to face her daughter's scary journey as a single parent. Teena has felt the pains of loneliness, financial strain, fear, and sheer exhaustion, but she has survived and is an inspiration to many.

Teena's most pronounced coping skill is humor. During some of her toughest days, I recall receiving phone calls or messages from her about something hilarious that had happened amid the obvious struggle. Teena's ability to find humor in this scary and painful situation was vital to her resilience. She modeled how to abide in the pain and gave this gift to her daughters, who both have an equally enjoyable sense of humor.

Sylvana is a huge Taylor Swift fan. In the months prior to her liver transplant surgery, which took place when she was eight years old, Sylvana would often joke that she wanted a part of Taylor Swift's liver. She just knew she would become famous! Don't misunderstand—humor didn't cover up Sylvana's pain. She also had to face the possibility that she would die before the transplant. But humor kept her balanced and helped her cope. (By the way, thanks to Make-A-Wish Foundation, Sylvana had the opportunity to meet Taylor Swift following her surgery!)

After receiving the call for the transplant, young Sylvana, facing the surgery of a lifetime, screamed, "It's liver time!" She drew the logo for her favorite college sports team on her belly so that her surgeon (from a rival school) could enjoy a few laughs as well. And while this may seem like a simple strategy in coping with life's hurts, let's not forget that we know from Scripture that cheerfulness has healing qualities: "A cheerful heart is good medicine, but a crushed spirit dries up the bones" (Prov. 17:22).

We can't afford to have a broken spirit, regardless of our circumstances. Without cheer and an occasional belly laugh, we will invite additional suffering. And science agrees. Do a quick Google search and you'll be inundated with reports of scientific proof of the health benefits of laughter. It strengthens the immune system, protects the heart, diminishes physical pain and depressive symptoms, and is a perfect anecdote for anxiety and stress. Laughter also triggers the release of endorphins and oxytocin, the body's feel-good chemicals.[2] So amid your hurt, seek out laughter. Look for the lighter side. Allow yourself to have a good, hearty laugh. Laughing doesn't minimize your pain, but it does provide a nice break from the sorrow.

One word of caution: the chemicals released when you belly laugh also promote bonding and thus can promote an affair with the wrong person in the wrong context. Make sure you're laughing and bonding with the right people. As with any tool, proceed with care! No sense making things more complicated when you're trying to build resilience, right?

Obsess about Jesus

Obsess about Jesus, and do so unapologetically. Stay in God's Word, remembering it is the only offensive weapon we have in spiritual battle (see Eph. 6:17). During intense struggle and pain, it will be helpful to read numerous devotions throughout the day, because immersing yourself in God's Word may be the only thing that can adequately refresh your perspective. Have a study time in the morning to start the day and focus your thoughts in a healthy way, choosing to rejoice in the day God has laid out before you. Add another study time in the evening prior to bed, as nighttime can be exceptionally difficult. Reading a short devotion will help you redirect any destructive thoughts and aid in preparing you for sleep. Feel free to also check out other Scripture readings and inspirational studies throughout the day.

Keep in mind that deep despair often impacts concentration and memory, so don't go for an intense theological study. You may not even be able to read a full chapter at a time. A more realistic plan may be for you to study only a few verses at a time. And don't stress about memorizing Scripture. If you can memorize some verses, great. But if your brain is too foggy, then this is the perfect time to utilize the tool of Christian meditation, which simply means you take a single verse and meditate on it one word at a time. Allow each word to come alive. Matthew 11:28 is a perfect place to start: "Come to me, all you who are weary and burdened, and I will give you rest." Close your eyes and dwell on each word of this invitation; imagine yourself fully responding to the offer. Allow yourself to be still before Him. This is what Christian meditation looks like, and it is good for the soul. Jesus is the Rock who will get you through this storm, and this is the time to obsess about Him!

Evaluate and Adjust

Your new normal may bring additional demands. You may have extra responsibilities, or you may find that the emotional toll is so great that you can barely accomplish the minimal demands of everyday life. Anytime we make an addition to our daily lives, we also must make a subtraction. Your struggles may be taking up significant space in your schedule during this season, so you will have to eliminate other things to create space. Evaluate your stress level. Evaluate your availability of time. Evaluate your physical demands. Consider nonnegotiable responsibilities. Intentionally reduce unnecessary stressors. You may need to relinquish some work-related or church-related responsibilities. Narrow down your to-do list to the must-do list, and do only the things on that list until your season passes. Extend yourself some grace. Consider your situation and what you would expect of someone else experiencing a similar trial. Give yourself the same grace you would extend to others, and remember that this is only a season. Better seasons are to come, and you will have the opportunity to evaluate and adjust once more after this harsh one passes.

Journal

Journaling is not helpful for everyone, but for those it does help, it is significantly impactful. Journaling is an effective tool because it allows us to get our troubles out of our heads and onto paper. For this reason, it helps us acknowledge our suffering, an important strategy for building resilience. So if you feel you are stuck, journaling may help push you along.

I do suggest a different form of journaling than you may have been previously taught. Often, we are instructed that journaling is an opportunity to vent. And while that can be true, if venting is all we do, then journaling will not be helpful and can potentially even be destructive. Journaling must also involve an acknowledgment of where God is working, praise in the midst of the storm, and recognition of gratitude. Remember, sometimes this will be mindful gratitude. We'll talk more in the next chapter about how to see where God is working, but for now, know that your journaling needs to be hope-focused or it will not be helpful in your tough journey. Experiment with journaling with this new focus and notice the refreshing influence it has on your perspective. Once you begin to journal, it may be helpful to look back at your writings on discouraging days.

See Your Physician

Perhaps your suffering is physical and you are tired of visiting doctors' offices. If that is the case, then you probably feel as though you are living your life confined to stale medical walls, and you yearn for the day you can walk away from this season. So this next bit of advice may not apply to you. However, if your hurt is emotional or relational, I would prescribe a trip to the doctor. Why? Because you don't want to miss any physiological issues that can complicate your resilience. A sluggish thyroid, a vitamin deficiency, or even issues with blood pressure or blood sugar can complicate your ability to bounce back from life's hurts. So if you haven't had a full physical in the last year or two, this is the perfect time for a checkup. Your physical well-being directly affects your resilience, and ensuring physical health is a basic part of self-care.

Exercise

The health benefits of exercise are mind-boggling. I'm sure your physician has challenged you more than once to add exercise into your lifestyle. Though you probably didn't expect to see an exercise push in a book about suffering, I cannot leave it out. For all the physical health benefits that exercise produces, the list of mental health benefits is equally impressive. Thirty minutes of exercise causes the human body to release those happy chemicals I mentioned earlier—endorphins and oxytocin—so a brisk walk, a jog, or a workout at the gym can almost instantly boost mood, alleviate anxiety, clear some of the brain fog, and minimize stress. Exercise helps buffer some of the destructive coping skills we're vulnerable to when we are struggling and aids in fighting the insomnia that sometimes plagues us in our trials.

Please know that one workout won't do—you need to make exercise part of your weekly schedule. I realize you may not feel like exercising and are probably fatigued, but exercise will boost your energy level. Give it a try. I would be extremely surprised if you didn't feel at least some boost. Of course, check with your physician to make sure you are healthy enough for exercise. When they give you the green light, get busy building some resilience with physical activity!

Get Adequate Nutrition

When you are emotionally broken, it seems you either have no appetite or crave the worst foods on the face of the planet. You reach for the carbs and sugars. You eat your weight in ice cream and potato chips but continue to drown in your sorrow. Or you don't eat at all. Both of these extremes are unwise. If there's ever been a time in your life when you absolutely should eat nutritiously, this, in the midst of your suffering, is the time. Your immune system is compromised from the stress of your emotional pain, so you must treat your body carefully. Think of food as medicine for your soul. A diet rich in carbs and sugars will create instability in your blood sugars, which will also create instability in your emotions. Instead, focus on consuming foods that are close to the earth. Think of healthy nutrition as consuming God-made foods, not man-made foods. Foods without a label—or at least foods with recognizable ingredients.

If you find yourself emotionally eating or bingeing when you are not hungry, then look for a replacement for that poor coping skill. Make yourself a list of alternatives to the binge and keep your list handy. This list is your "toolbox," and you always need to keep a toolbox close by. Your list could include things like taking a walk, calling a friend, gardening, reading a devotional, visiting a neighbor, or playing with a pet. If you allow yourself to be distracted by a healthy coping skill for just ten or fifteen minutes, the craving will pass. Overeating to soothe or forget your emotions will complicate your suffering, creating more struggles for you to later climb your way out of. If the opposite is true and you have lost your appetite, discipline yourself to eat small, frequent meals throughout the day. You will have to make deliberate choices in your nutrition, but you will be glad you did. Your physical body will be healthier, your immune system will be stronger, your blood sugars will be more stable, your weight is more likely to reach a normal range, and your mood will be more stable. Those are some wonderful incentives to healthy nutrition!

Sleep

Just as your trials affect your appetite, they also impact your sleep. Sleep represents roughly one-third of our lives and is a basic but absolutely vital ingredient to your physical health and resilience. The average person requires anywhere from seven to nine hours of restful sleep per night, with children requiring more. In the midst of a struggle, you may be depressed and tempted to sleep your days away to escape the emotional pain you are feeling. However, sleeping too much only prolongs your denial and postpones your opportunities to build resilience. All the pain will still be waiting for you when you wake up, so sleeping through your pain is not a helpful coping skill.

Maybe insomnia is your biggest challenge. Worry sometimes keeps you awake, but you eventually need sound sleep to heal and recover. Sleep deprivation makes it more challenging to manage your emotions. If you are struggling with insomnia, begin with some basic sleep strategies and see if your sleep improves. Eliminate caffeine and long naps during the day. Avoid screen time, exercise, and eating two hours prior to bed. Make sure you remove night-lights. Ensure that your bed is designated for sleep and not someplace you go to during the day to read a book or rest. Your doctor can even recommend some natural supplements that are effective sleep aids. If you are already utilizing these sleep strategies but are still experiencing unimproved insomnia, I encourage you to speak with your physician. Sound sleep is essential to bouncing back from the hurts of life.

Breathe

Breathe deeply. Breathe slowly. Pay attention to your breathing. Thank God that you have breath. Awareness and control of this simple aspect of your survival is grounding when life is chaotic. Slowing your breathing can provide measurable relief from your anxiety and calm you when your fears get the best of you.

Write a Letter

While letter writing may not seem to be a very sophisticated self-care tool, it can be powerful in helping you get unstuck. If you are bombarded with strong, negative emotions at the thought or mention of an individual who has caused you hurt, then unforgiveness may be keeping you stuck. Oftentimes, letter writing is a catalyst to release that unforgiveness. Let's be clear: I am not suggesting you send a foul letter to someone who has hurt you. *In fact, I'm not suggesting you send a letter at all.* A letter is simply designed to give you the opportunity to see, in writing, the hurt you have felt as well as your decision to forgive this person.

Perhaps the person you have the most difficult time forgiving is yourself. You are suffering because of the consequences of your choices. In this case, a couple of letters are in order. Write the first letter as if it is from God to you. Write down brief facts regarding the choices you regret. Then focus your writing on God's forgiveness of you and Scripture passages that serve as evidence of His forgiveness. Next, write another letter, but this time address it from you to God, in response to the first letter. Acknowledge the mess you've made. Then acknowledge

154

the forgiveness you've been offered, and write down your acceptance of that gift.

What do you do with a letter you have written to someone? Only in rare circumstances, and with the leading of God and the counsel of an objective and wise pastor or counselor, would I recommend sending a letter you have written to someone else. This exercise is not intended for others; it is for your purposes. Consequently, the most powerful and helpful thing to do with the letter is to: (1) Save it in a safe place so you have it to reflect on in future times of struggle. You may need the reminder of the work you've already done in forgiveness. (2) Burn it and pray with thanksgiving while you watch all the bitterness symbolically released as the letter turns to ashes. (3) Shred it and add it to the soil in a flower garden. Watch over time as something beautiful grows where your letter was left. (4) Get creative. The options are endless. The symbolism of what you do with the letter is powerful in your healing process and gives you a tangible reminder of the freedom you gained at that particular time.

Guard and Postpone

Don't get me wrong. I'm not an advocate of procrastination. But I do advocate postponing. In an attempt to dull the pain during seasons of suffering, we are sometimes vulnerable to impulsive decisions that have long-lasting consequences. Guard yourself against radical decisions that may make a radical impact. If you are working through a significant struggle, this may not be the appropriate time to buy a new home, change jobs, move to a new city, or purchase a different vehicle. Impulsive choices made when you are in deep despair often come back to bite you. If at all possible, postpone major decisions until you are in a better frame of mind.

Seek Wise Counsel

Being a lone ranger in a trial is not a good idea. Remember, your trial is new terrain and may call for additional expertise. This is an appropriate time to seek wise counsel, which you will find to be a helpful, and often necessary, tool for self-care. Some of the wisest people I've ever met are those who reached out for counsel and coaching during a tough storm of life. Professionals in every field can more adequately guide you than you may be able to guide yourself. Depending on your situation, you may want to consult with one or more of the following: a professional counselor, an attorney, a financial advisor, or a physician. Seek expertise from the professionals most equipped to meet the specific needs of your particular situation. This will aid in building your resilience. Remember the insight of Proverbs 13:20: "Walk with the wise and become wise." Seek out the wisdom of others and walk with them through this valley.

Miscellaneous Self-Care Nuggets

Self-care can mean different things for different people, so be creative and do what works for you! Cuddle with a beloved pet. Light a candle. Take a warm shower or bubble bath. Hike to the top of a mountain. Sit by a peaceful brook. Visit the ocean. Get a pedicure. Take a stroll through your favorite thrift store. Play a round of golf with some friends. Yes, these things might seem superficial. No, these things don't take away your hurt. However, they do offer a temporary sense of peace and give you something simple to look forward to. And you need nuggets of peace amid your pain.

Persevere

Jimmy Valvano is a household name to North Carolina State University fans. Jimmy V. is known for not only his success in leading a Cinderella-story basketball team in the 1980s but also his brave battle with cancer. Less than two months before his death in April 1993, Valvano gave a famous and inspiring acceptance speech after receiving the inaugural Arthur Ashe Courage and Humanitarian Award at the ESPY Awards. Why has this speech touched so many people? Because when we are suffering, we are tempted to throw in the towel. We are weary. We reach a point where we feel we cannot fight anymore; we're done. Jimmy, his body covered in tumors, gave an enthusiastic directive in that speech: "Don't give up. . . . Don't ever give up!" These words continue to inspire and now also serve as the motto for the V Foundation for Cancer Research, established in Jimmy's honor.

If you want resilience, giving up is simply not an option. You must persevere. As Paul writes, "I press on toward the goal to win the prize for which God has called me heavenward in Christ Jesus" (Phil. 3:14). Don't give up prematurely. In fact, don't give up at all, until you are certain that God is ready for you to give up. Press on. This trial is not a sprint; it is a marathon. You must stay in the race. You must *finish* the race.

To sum it up, trauma and suffering pose a threat to your emotional well-being, your spiritual life, your relationships, and even your physical health. In fact, the stress caused by a traumatic situation even jeopardizes your immune system and lowers your defenses against illness and disease. Self-care is vitally important to your resilience in the face of such tremendous struggle. The practical tools in this chapter aid you in surviving a challenging situation and in setting the foundation for bouncing back from life's hurts. You will find some tools are absolutely necessary for your coping; others will simply be extra helps. Either way, you will have to be intentional. These tools do not come automatically. In fact, you will probably resist some of them altogether. Push through that resistance and know that in doing so you are bouncing back from the hurts that have kept you stuck, and you are beginning to build resilience!

> ### *Victory Verse*
>
> Be still, and know that I am God.
> Psalm 46:10

Application Questions

1. Consider some difficult hurdles you conquered in your past. How did you take care of yourself then? Were there some specific tools that were most helpful? How can you use those tools in your current situation?

2. Where are you currently lacking in regard to self-care? What practical steps do you need to take to help you cope more effectively and assist you in building resilience?

3. Consider some of the most resilient people you've met. How did they take care of themselves in practical ways? What can you learn from their behavior?

4. Today is the day to start focusing more intently on taking care of yourself. Where will you start?

PART 3

Now that You Are Unstuck... Learning to Thrive

If you have been closely following these proactive chapters and applying the practical lessons to your life, then you are likely unstuck! If you're not completely unstuck, then you probably have made at least *some* progress in this journey. Congratulations! Getting unstuck is a blessing. It feels great to be free of the restriction of intense pain and despair. But you don't have to stop here. If you settle for simply being unstuck, you miss the experience of thriving, of purpose, of integrating your experience into your life story. Those who thrive despite their suffering have a few additional secrets. So if you find even greater freedom and joy enticing, then let's continue this journey together. We don't just want to be unstuck. We want to be resilient!

Seeing Your Experience
in Light of the Big Picture

My dear friend and colleague Patty has the most severe case of lupus I have ever witnessed. Lupus is sometimes called the "great imitator" because it is a confusing disease that wreaks havoc on the body, comes in unpredictable blows, and often mimics other diseases or injuries. Those who live with chronic illnesses, such as lupus, endure a roller-coaster life—sometimes enjoying remission, sometimes suffering a full-blown attack. It is not an easy journey. It hurts physically. It challenges emotionally. It tests spiritually. And no cure exists.

Patty is an amazingly resilient woman. Though lupus puts up a great fight at times, she has learned to manage it with a pure and powerful eternal perspective that is a rarity, even among those of us who proclaim Christ. Patty considers Psalm 34 a bedrock of hope. "I will bless the LORD at all times; his praise shall continually be in my mouth" (v. 1 ESV). Because having blisters in the mouth and nose is an ongoing struggle for lupus sufferers, this particular verse renews her strength. "I will praise the Lord at all times," Patty says, "even with the blisters. His praise shall be in my mouth. No illness can take away my ability to magnify Him."

Unfortunately, blisters have been the least of Patty's struggles. Lupus has attacked her eyes, her connective tissues, and her bones. Lupus also attacked her brain, making speaking and walking difficult for months. She couldn't read because her thinking, comprehension, and vision were dramatically affected. Her husband would read the Bible aloud to her. Patty reflects on that time, saying, "I knew that even during the dark of night, I was not hidden from His sight. Everything about me was open to His eyes, and His eyes are full of love. In the dark, you can feel that incredible love even more intensely."

Most recently, Patty experienced what appeared to be symptoms of the dreaded Lou Gehrig's disease (ALS). Tests were inconclusive for a full year but finally revealed that it was just the great imitator at work in her body once again. This time of waiting was particularly difficult physically, emotionally, and spiritually. One week during our staff prayer time, Patty poured out her heart. This pouring was a glimpse into the root of her resilience. "The gavel keeps coming down. My world is crushing," Patty said. She appreciated more deeply than ever before the desperation recorded in Habakkuk 3:17–19:

> Though the fig tree does not bud and there are no grapes on the vines, though the olive crop fails and the fields produce no food, though there are no sheep in the pen and no cattle in the stalls, yet I will rejoice in the LORD, I will be joyful in God my Savior. The Sovereign LORD is my strength; he makes my feet like the feet of a deer, he enables me to tread on the heights.

In a sincere and gentle voice, she passionately went on to say, "I cling to the *relationship* when the gavel falls. I can't cling to the promises right now. I don't know what is going to happen. It's just where I am. But God is my strength. The God of my salvation. I cling to Him. I cling to the *relationship*, because my relationship with Him is my strength."

Our trials and struggles expose us, revealing our true beliefs and our sincerest relationships. This trial in Patty's life revealed both her resilience and the source of her hope. You see, to Patty, hope is not just anything. Hope is a *person*. And that person is Christ, Who trumps every other fabricated hope our world can offer. A relationship with Christ is available not only to Patty. It is also available to you and to me. A relationship with Christ is the foundation of forming an eternal perspective, which we will discuss more in-depth later in the chapter.

Does God Really Care about My Suffering?

"Ladies and gentlemen, please rise and remove your caps for the singing of the national anthem." We've all heard this announcement at a ball game or celebration. But do you ever wonder why you're standing? Standing is considered appropriate in many situations. We give a standing ovation for someone who has just sung or performed marvelously or is being recognized for an achievement. We stand for a bride as she enters the room to greet her groom. We stand for a judge as they enter the courtroom. We stand for a family as they are escorted into a church or funeral home just prior to the funeral of a loved one. We stand during the Pledge of Allegiance. We stand for the singing of the "Hallelujah Chorus." Standing is a symbolic expression of our respect. Our honor. Our undivided attention.

Recently, I discovered something about standing in relation to Jesus. My pastor, referencing the stoning of Stephen as recorded in Acts 7, spoke of Jesus standing in heaven: "But Stephen, full of the Holy Spirit, looked up to heaven and saw the glory of God, and

Jesus standing at the right hand of God" (v. 55). I was puzzled; I had always thought of Jesus taking His place *seated* at the right hand of the Father. Though I have probably read this verse many times before, I never caught the significance of Jesus's posture. He was doing something unusual, for at no other time in Scripture is Christ described as standing at God's right hand; all other references are to Him sitting. Something brought Jesus to His feet. Perhaps it was that He wanted to give His full attention to Stephen's suffering. Perhaps it was much like a standing ovation, an expression of love and respect for Stephen. Perhaps he was standing as an expression of honor. Perhaps Christ was welcoming Stephen into His presence. Perhaps He was standing in anger at the injustice Stephen was facing. Perhaps standing was a defensive stance—a standing up for Stephen. Perhaps it was judgment. While I can't begin to explain the full rationale of Christ's act of standing, I do know it was significant.

Oftentimes, when we suffer, we feel that God is distant. Unengaged. Unaware. Silent. We may be confused by what seems to be His lack of attention. I am comforted by this Scripture passage, aren't you? When Christ seems silent, it may just be that He is standing—full of love and respect. Your suffering, indeed, has His full attention. He cares. He is your defender. If you are struggling today, meditate on this image of Christ standing at the right hand of the Father, brought to His feet to focus on you.

The Circle

To benefit from an eternal perspective, we must first accept that God really does care about our suffering. Reflecting on His care is an important ingredient in resilience. Now let me walk you through an exercise I call "the circle," as it helps us to visually recognize where we stand with God and our suffering.

Close your eyes and imagine, in your mind's eye, a large circle. Inside that circle are key words that identify areas of your life you routinely bring to God, meaning you regularly converse with Him regarding these areas. You experience His comfort and guidance regarding these areas. Now on a piece of paper, draw a circle and write these words on the inside.

Sometimes our greatest wounds and most intense suffering aren't brought into that circle. They are untouchable. We feel either shame or fear about approaching God with these struggles. Where is your hurt? Your pain? Are they inside the circle? Are you regularly communicating with God about your wounds? Or are they outside the circle—as far away as possible?

Until we muster the courage to bring our suffering into the circle, into our relationship with Christ, we will miss the opportunity to experience great relief. For example, after I encouraged a client to have his first conversation with God about the childhood molestation that had plagued him for decades, he reported being surprised to experience a calmness, a peace. This man's circle had been relatively full. He had a close relationship with God, spent time in His Word daily, and communicated with God about many areas of his life. But he had been silent about this one significant area, and the silence had been deafening. But not anymore. Let this client's courage inspire you to bring your suffering into the circle that is your relationship with God. Remember, He *does* care. He already knows. And He wants to talk.

A Shadow versus an Eternal Perspective

You may be suffering from a terminal illness. Or you may be facing some other form of emotional or physical pain. God speaks profound truth to our hurts through His Word, so let's take a look at an often-quoted passage that will encourage you to view your situation from a different angle, in light of the big picture. Reading His Word and agreeing with His viewpoint are imperative for gaining an eternal perspective.

Psalm 23:4 says, "Yea, though I walk through the valley of the shadow of death, I will fear no evil; for You are with me; Your rod and Your staff, they comfort me" (NKJV). Some people relate this verse to death. I say it's not about death at all. It's about a shadow! There's a big difference between death and a shadow, wouldn't you say? Which perspective will you take? Are you entering death? Or a shadow? Is God's rod painful? Or does it protect and comfort? Your willingness to consider God's point of view on your situation determines your hesitations, or your ease, at leaning in to the inevitable storms of life. If you are facing a trial bigger than yourself, remember that it is only a shadow. Pray that God will reveal His eternal perspective, which will reframe your suffering, comfort your fears, guide you through this tough season, and build your resilience.

When we consider that our lives on earth are as quick as a blink of an eye compared to eternity in heaven, we can acknowledge that tough experiences within that blink of time have less significance than we tend to give them. If the blink were all we had in terms of quality of life, then our trials would be a really big deal. But we have more than a blink. When we contemplate the weight of our struggles in light of an eternal perspective, some of the angst of our earthly experience is diminished. This eternal perspective of genuine hope is a refreshing and necessary reality check for a thriving experience in suffering.

We must refuse to place too much emphasis on temporary suffering, on pain that will be allowed to continue only for the season that is this life on earth. On the contrary, we must insist on giving more credit to God's point of view—a permanent hope—and see our shadows for what they truly are.

How Do I Apply an Eternal Perspective to My Suffering?

The prophet Jeremiah serves as a great example of how to apply an eternal perspective to suffering. In Lamentations, Jeremiah acknowledges his suffering. In fact, he is pretty thorough in laying out just how bad things are. In the first eighteen verses of chapter 3, Jeremiah discloses his afflictions, his physical sufferings, his isolation, his discouragements, his hardships, and his despair, and his pain is clearly intense. And then there is the "Yes, but . . ." we identified as being so incredibly helpful in preventing us from getting stuck. Jeremiah writes:

> I remember my affliction and my wandering, the bitterness and the gall. I well remember them, and my soul is downcast within me. Yet this I call to mind and therefore I have hope: Because of the LORD's great love we are not consumed, for his compassions never fail. They are new every morning; great is your faithfulness. I say to myself, "The LORD is my portion; therefore I will wait for him." The LORD is good to those whose hope is in him, to the one who seeks him; it is good to wait quietly for the salvation of the LORD. (vv. 19–26)

Jeremiah continues on, at length, shifting his focus beyond his immediate suffering.

Remember our discussions about how important it is to tell the whole story? Jeremiah clearly tells the whole story, and this eternal aspect is the most important part of Jeremiah's story. The same is true for you and me. The eternal truth is not just a nice add-on. It is the climax of the story. It is the main character. It is the punch line. It is the entire theme. We simply cannot ignore the eternal picture in the story of our suffering.

How Do I Keep an Eternal Perspective When I Am Suffering in the Here and Now?

Connecting with others is important. But your relationship with God is the most important relationship in both the good times and the bad times. It's one thing to have a momentary glimpse at the big picture, but to maintain an eternal viewpoint you must stay connected to that eternal relationship. Because you are struggling, you often have tunnel vision and get sucked into the here and now. Some degree of that will be normal and unavoidable. But you must facilitate allowing your hurts to direct you to God rather than away from Him. In the previous chapter, we talked about obsessing about Jesus. Obsessing doesn't mean you are a religious freak or that you're "so heavenly minded you're no earthly good" or that you cannot even function on earth. Obsessing means you gain a perspective that helps you cope, helps you better understand the curveballs thrown at you, helps you see your suffering from a different angle. It keeps you balanced in a healthy way. It gives you greater confidence, and therefore boldness, to move along in your tough journey. Spend time in His Word. Digesting large doses of Scripture may be challenging, so focus on verses that speak to your heart. Listening is half of a relationship, so take the time to just be still in His presence. Be with Him. Allow Him to be with you! Let Him battle for you. "The Lord will fight for you; you need only to be still" (Exod. 14:14). Remember, He is the ultimate builder of resilience. You just need to cooperate.

What if I Experience Unbelief?

This all sounds great, but I'm not sure I believe. I want to believe. I think I believe. But sometimes it is so hard when I can't see ahead. We've all had some of these thoughts in the midst of our pain. Unfortunately, unbelief can become a habit that keeps us stuck, and the only solution is simply choosing to believe. Faith. We cry out with our brothers and sisters in Christ, "I do believe; help me overcome my unbelief!" (Mark 9:24). In times of unbelief, ground yourself in Who you know God to be. Ground yourself in those aspects of God's character in which you do not doubt. In which you do not struggle. Maybe you struggle with His protection, but you can ground yourself in the fact that He is your Creator. Or that He is your Savior. Or that He is your Comforter. When you struggle, force yourself to reflect not only on your doubt but also on your areas of confidence. Reflect often on those areas of genuine belief and assurance for help in times of doubt and uncertainty. Frequently, we trust God with our salvation but struggle to believe Him in our suffering. Remember, He remains the same. Whether you turn to Him regarding your eternal soul or your temporary pain, He remains the same God throughout.

I realize that some of you reading this chapter have never believed. You have never trusted Christ for your salvation. You are not a Christian. I urge you at this moment, as you read this book, to make a decision about Christ. The benefits of an eternal perspective are out of reach without a trusting relationship with Him. And that relationship starts with acknowledging He is who He proclaims Himself to be—the Son of God who came to restore us to relationship with God. Thank Him for his sacrifice on the cross. Ask forgiveness for a debt you can never repay. And make a choice to trust Him to lead your life. "For God so loved the world that he gave his one and only Son, that whoever believes in him shall not perish but have eternal life" (John 3:16). He is the only path to eternal peace, and He is the only path to genuine resilience this side of eternity. I pray that you boldly make Him both Savior and Lord of your life.

What if I Never Get Relief from My Suffering?

Faith means being sure of something not yet fully experienced. "Now faith is confidence in what we hope for and assurance about what we do not see" (Heb. 11:1). When we struggle, we experience many unknowns. We can't see into the future, but we all have certain beliefs about what could or should happen. We cling to either a catastrophic belief that has no hope or a faith-based belief that hopes in something that has not yet come to pass. Hebrews 11 is an encouragement for those whose suffering may not be relieved. The chapter reminds us of spiritual heroes who were credited for their tremendous faith: Abel, Enoch, Noah, Abraham, Isaac, Jacob, Joseph, Moses, Rahab . . . and the list goes on.

> All these people were still living by faith when they died. They did not receive the things promised; they only saw them and welcomed them from a distance, admitting that they were foreigners and strangers on earth. People who say such things show that they are looking for a country of their own. (vv. 13–14)

When I read these verses from Hebrews, I find myself taking a deep breath. These heroes were living by faith when they died. They didn't receive "the things promised" before their deaths. They died relying on hope beyond this world. I don't want my realization to be true, but it is: some suffering will not be relinquished, at least not this side of eternity. Our world is getting darker and darker. Threats of terrorism. Reports of natural disasters. Disease. Times are progressing, and suffering seems to be more widespread and tangible than I've seen previously in my lifetime. It's becoming more and more obvious that our hope simply can't reside in anything this temporary life has to offer.

My father-in-law has endured four decades of physical suffering. He has survived more medical obstacles than seem possible. A heart attack at age thirty-one that threatened to take his life but didn't. Another heart attack years later. A heart transplant two decades later. Life-threatening pneumonia on multiple occasions. Numerous blood clots. Diabetes. An aneurism. Reccurring cancer. A stroke. An amputation. Doctors have advised him more times than I can count that death is imminent and he needs to get his affairs in order. His affairs have been in order for decades! More likely than ever before, however, it seems God is bringing his time on this earth to an end. Nearly forty years after the massive heart attack of his thirties, his body is barely still functioning; medical appointments, procedures, and treatments dominate nearly all the time he has left. During a recent conversation, he and I spoke honestly about the reality he is up against. He may never fully overcome the effects of his most recent stroke or beat the reccurring cancer. No indications point to the relief of his suffering in this lifetime. He said to me, "The only hope I have left is eternity."

Isn't that true of us all? *Our only authentic hope is eternity.*

To Die Is Gain?

"To live is Christ and to die is gain" (Phil. 1:21). Paul's words inspire us to live fully in the time God has given us on this earth. Unshackled. Unrestrained. Unstuck. Bouncing back from the hurts of this temporary life. Let's reject anything that hinders His being glorified and never forget that our ultimate gain is in death, for we will live forever with Christ.

Listen, friends! We are in a win-win situation. No matter our trials. Despite our struggles. Living is Christ and dying is gain. That is a worldview that not only breaks oppression but also builds resilience. When you live by genuine faith, you simply cannot be permanently trapped by life's hurts. Much like a buoy tossed around and pushed down by stormy waters, eventually you will rise to the surface!

What Is the Purpose of Suffering?

As I was writing this chapter, I looked through a decades-old notebook of notes written by my father-in-law. The theme of his writings was suffering. One profound statement rose from the pages: "God, help this circumstance to change me before you remove it." What a bold prayer! But does God really use tough circumstances purposefully? You better believe He does!

Understanding the purpose in suffering, from God's perspective, is imperative for resilience. Remember, God ultimately provides our resilience. We simply cooperate.

So what does God say about the purpose of suffering? James writes this: "Consider it pure joy, my brothers and sisters, whenever you face trials of many kinds, because you know that the testing of your faith produces perseverance. Let perseverance finish its work so that you may be mature and complete, not lacking anything" (James 1:2–4). Read those verses again, slowly. Trials stretch our faith. They produce perseverance (it doesn't come naturally). Our suffering matures and completes us. Our struggles make us whole. So suffering is not only a normal part of the human existence; God also makes it beneficial.

Many times in my office, when a client has first disclosed a painful experience, I have leaned forward and offered a promise: "There will be a day when you will be grateful for this pain. You will never, ever want to experience it again. And you will be thankful you are out of this season of suffering. But if you cooperate with God, you will be grateful for everything this season will teach you and all the ways it will strengthen you. That day won't be tomorrow or even next month. But as long as you cooperate with Him, that day will come." Time and time again, I've had people come back to share their gratitude for their experience, though they didn't necessarily believe me in the midst of the intense pain. God finishes what He starts, and you too will feel gratitude—not for the trial or the suffering or the injustice or the regrets but for the growth. Why? Because you don't grow any other way!

When we view our struggles in light of an eternal perspective, seeking to understand where God is at work and how He will use our suffering to refine us and glorify Himself, we are positioned to bounce back from our hurts and rewarded with long-lasting resilience.

Viticulture: Producing Fruit from Our Trials

Our staff enjoys a devotional time together each week. One recent week we had the pleasure of studying viticulture, the science and production of grapes and winemaking. I know what you're thinking: *Why is a counseling center studying vineyards and wines? Even more concerning, why is this part of their devotion time?* Give me just a minute, and I think you'll understand. You might even read something that applies to the struggles you are facing in life. Here is your sixty-second lesson in viticulture.

Quality grapes used in fine wines grow in mountain ranges with steep, rugged hillsides. These vines must be exposed to direct sunlight, and the soil in which the vines grow in must have good drainage. Also, these vines must *continuously struggle* to produce good fruit. The struggle is of utmost importance. The best grapes come from vines with roots that are forced to grow deep into the soil. These grapevines also shouldn't be grown in fertile soil. Vines grown in rich, fertilized soil have roots that spread too easily and too quickly, causing them to be shallow and resulting in poor fruit with little flavor. A vine that struggles produces fewer grapes, but they are better quality. To force some struggle in an effort to produce better fruit, the vine is given a minimal amount of water through the use of controlled irrigation. The vine is also trellised to control its shape, with the purpose of maximizing sun exposure. Lastly, the vine is pruned not in a harsh or destructive way but by hand, gently, and with delicate tools. The gardener prunes with purpose, removing some branches for more sun exposure and harvesting the green, immature bunches of grapes to increase the yield and quality of the fruit.

So what is the purpose of this short introduction to viticulture? Let's look at the discussion of the vine and the branches in John 15:

> I am the true vine, and my Father is the gardener. He cuts off every branch in me that bears no fruit, while every branch that does bear fruit he prunes so that it will be even more fruitful. . . . Remain in me, as I also remain in you. No branch can bear fruit by itself; it must remain in the vine. Neither can you bear fruit unless you remain in me. I am the vine; you are the branches. If you remain in me and I in you, you will bear much fruit; apart from me you can do nothing. If you do not remain in me, you are like a branch that is thrown away and withers; such branches are picked up, thrown into the fire and burned. If you remain in me and my words remain in you, ask whatever you wish, and it will be done for you. This is to my Father's glory, that you bear much fruit, showing yourselves to be my disciples. (vv. 1–2, 4–8)

Today you may struggle. You may feel you are being pruned. You are digging deep just trying to survive! Remember, you are a branch. *Remain in your Vine, and trust your Gardener.* The Master Gardener has great purpose in His pruning! He wants you to produce fantastic fruit. Allow the pruning to make you healthier, more focused, more productive, and more purposeful. Allow God to use the struggles in your life to remove things that are not good for you or honoring to Him. Allow fruit to come from your trials and difficulties. Just cooperate. Much like a pearl begins with an irritant, your suffering at the hands of an unwelcomed trial can bring something amazing into your life. Yes, it takes time, but a trial produces beautiful things.

God allows (and sometimes even initiates) discomfort to produce remarkable results. So today let's consider welcoming our struggles. Let's look for fruit. Let's look for purpose. The most memorable outcomes can be experienced only through great struggle, so let no struggle go to waste.

What Can Prevent My Trial from Producing Fruit?

One thing can prevent your trials from producing fruit: sin. I am struck by David's profound words: "Look on my affliction and my distress and take away all my sins" (Ps. 25:18). David, in distress, asked God to be more aggressive in removing his sin than in relieving his suffering. He asked God to "look on" his affliction but to "take away" his sin. Usually, we switch those two, asking primarily for relief from our distress. We are much more acquainted with the sorrow of our suffering than the power of our sin. However, we are to take our sorrows and our sins to the same place and apply to them the same hierarchy of importance David used. God is more concerned about our sin than our suffering. Why? Because suffering produces fruit. Sin produces destruction. So confess any unacknowledged sin to God and ask Him to aggressively remove it.

God Might Produce Fruit, but Can He Ever Heal Me?

The storms of life change us. But change doesn't have to be catastrophic. When we maintain an eternal perspective, we position ourselves to overcome any obstacles in our path. I have seen, more times than I can count, oppressions lifted, addictions overcome, depression halted, eating disorders silenced, marriages restored, and hope found. That is welcomed change! My observations of God's desires are consistent with the words of the prophet Isaiah:

> To bestow on them a crown of beauty instead of ashes, the oil of joy instead of mourning, and a garment of praise instead of a spirit of despair. They will be called oaks of righteousness, a planting of the LORD for the display of his splendor. They will rebuild the ancient ruins and restore the places long devastated; they will renew the ruined cities that have been devastated for generations. (61:3–4)

God *can* bring you out of your pit! He *can* free you from being stuck. And He *can* cause you to bounce back from your hurt. He proclaims freedom, release from darkness, comfort in sadness, beauty instead of ashes, joy instead of mourning, and praise instead of despair. He rebuilds and renews what is ruined. He restores what is devastated. What's more? God can indeed replace your suffering with resilience! Resilience is more than just healing. Resilience comes when God takes a painful circumstance in your life and not only heals you but also makes you even stronger than you were prior to the struggle. Get this: "And the God of all grace, who called you to his eternal glory in Christ, after you have suffered a little while, will himself restore you and make you strong, firm and steadfast" (1 Pet. 5:10). Restored. Strong. Firm. Steadfast. Sounds like resilience, doesn't it?

Hold on to your hat, because in the next chapter you will be introduced to genuine resilience. How to be productive, fruitful, purposeful, and healthy. I promise you will be inspired by some of my most admired heroes in resilience!

Victory Verse

The LORD himself goes before you and will be with you; he will never leave you nor forsake you. Do not be afraid; do not be discouraged.

Deuteronomy 31:8

Application Questions

1. Consider your painful trial in light of an eternal perspective. What do you see when you look at your trial from this angle?

2. What is the importance of this perspective regarding your particular trial? How does this viewpoint impact your ability to cope?

3. "Be still and know that I am God" (Ps. 46:10). *Be still* means to stop. *Know* means to acknowledge. Allow yourself some downtime to reflect on this verse. You don't always have to be busy running from suffering. Enjoy being intentionally still. Reflect on knowing God, not just your suffering. After you have finished, think about what impact this time of reflection might have? Did it provide a different perspective on your struggles? How?

4. Do you struggle with unbelief? If so, how does it affect your ability to bounce back from hurt? How do you plan to address this struggle?

5. We discussed God's use of the description of the vine and the branches. How does this correlation apply to your suffering?

6. Purpose and fruit in a trial are God's work. How can you best cooperate with Him in your current situation? What fruit has already come from your trial?

7. Look up a few definitions of the word *resilient*. Write down your favorite.

Now imagine your picture beside that definition. Imagine it is a description of you. Meditate on what God can do in your life as a direct result of the hurts you have endured. Do not limit His ability to bring resilience into your life and your future!

Turning Suffering into Purpose

One of my favorite spiritual heroes of the Bible is Esther. Children who hear her story are attracted to the fact that she was a beautiful girl who became queen. I'm drawn to the fact that she was a woman who endured significant suffering but whose life portrays her purpose and her resilience more than her pain. Let's review some of the hurts she experienced and see if we can relate. (If you're not familiar with Esther's story, then I encourage you to pause here and read the book of Esther in the Old Testament. It will be time well spent. Esther's story is a made-for-the-big-screen adventure you don't want to miss.)

We know Esther was taken into captivity as a very young girl, along with many other Jews. By definition, captivity suggests force. She wasn't offered a choice. Wow. That's a heavy start. But, unfortunately, her situation didn't get happier. Esther was an orphan, raised by her cousin Mordecai. Though the Bible provides few other details, we can easily deduce that her childhood involved a lot of pain. Now fast-forward to her teen years. King Xerxes (who had just recently dethroned his queen for refusing to parade in front of him and a group of men) ordered young virgins to be brought into his harem, and "Esther was also taken" (Esther 2:8). This was no beauty pageant that Esther signed up for; this was a sex-trafficking case ordered by none other than the king himself. Esther was kidnapped! After a year of being in the harem, it was her time to go to the king. In other words, she was sent to the king to have sex with him. She lost her virginity in the king's experiment and would have been subjected to living with other concubines in the palace had he not chosen her to be queen. Indeed, she *was* selected to be queen, which might sound like the greatest thing ever, but this king was a jerk with an anger problem, probably an alcohol problem, and not a bit of respect for women. Esther became an inmate of the palace. Then, while she was queen, she learned that Haman, the king's right-hand man, planned to massacre her people.

That's a quick review of Esther's life. Clearly, despite being queen, Esther did not have an easy life! She didn't grow up with a silver spoon in her mouth. She didn't get her way. She didn't live life protected from pain. In fact, she endured trauma and tragedy. Hurt and suffering. Pain and fear. Loneliness and isolation. Esther's hurts were similar to yours and mine. But she had uncommon resilience.

What is the evidence of Esther's resilience?

1. She managed to adapt to one situation after another. She didn't get stuck. Esther seemed to know how to make lemonade from her lemons. She replaced whining with gratitude. Though she would have had every right to, she never adopted a "woe is me" attitude. Instead, she had a gracious attitude that drew others to her and gave her credibility at a much-needed time (see Esther 2:8–9).

2. She was humble. She sought and took advice from others. She solicited and benefited from the wisdom of those around her. She wasn't a lone ranger (see vv. 15 and 20).

3. She acknowledged her suffering and expressed her fears—and then she faced them. It wasn't that she was without fear. It's that she was *with* courage. Simply processing her pain would have kept her stuck. When it was time to act, Esther took action (see 4:16).

4. She took care of herself physically. After fasting for three days, and probably not physically feeling well, she cleaned up, put on her royal robes, and approached the king (see 5:1).

5. She respected the roles of authority, even when respecting the corruption was difficult. Her respect and gratitude earned King Xerxes' attention. She was credible in the king's eyes (see 5:4–6).

6. Ultimately, Esther accepted that her journey had brought her to a point of additional suffering for a reason. As she faced the greatest fear of her life—the potential massacre of the nation she loved—she embraced Mordecai's challenge: "For if you remain silent at this time, relief and deliverance for the Jews will arise from another place, but you and your father's family will perish. And who knows but that you have come to your royal position for such a time as this?" (4:14).

For such a time as this . . . Those are powerful, purposeful words of resilience. Esther responded. She was willing to lay down her life for her friends and her nation. Esther was not a drama queen, even though she *was* queen. She focused on the task in front of her and had integrity in finishing what she had started. She embraced God's purpose in her suffering, and He used her mightily. When you read the entire book of Esther, you can see how thoroughly

Esther's resilience paid off. Long story short, her actions led to the rescue of an entire nation. Resilience has its rewards!

Esther exuded an inner beauty that enabled her to bounce back. She demonstrated what the New Testament refers to in Galatians 5:22–23 as the fruit of the Spirit: love, joy, peace, forbearance, kindness, goodness, faithfulness, gentleness, and self-control. She applied the fruit of the Spirit to her traumas and her obstacles— and she thrived. Esther is a hero, not because her life was easy but because it *wasn't* easy and she bounced back anyway.

Positioned for Purpose

Esther's story is motivating, isn't it? Her resilience is truly something to aspire to. In chapter 10, we discovered the benefits of maintaining an eternal perspective, so we are perfectly positioned to allow our suffering to be used for something meaningful. Transforming our pain into purpose begins with our intentional willingness to submit to the work of God.

True resilience comes when we allow our suffering to be used for a greater purpose, as this Scripture passage implies:

> Praise be to the God and Father of our Lord Jesus Christ, the Father of compassion and the God of all comfort, who comforts us in all our troubles, so that we can comfort those in any trouble with the comfort we ourselves receive from God. For just as we share abundantly in the sufferings of Christ, so also our comfort abounds through Christ. If we are distressed, it is for your comfort and salvation; if we are comforted, it is for your comfort, which produces in you patient endurance of the same sufferings we suffer. And our hope for you is firm, because we know that just as you share in our sufferings, so also you share in our comfort. (2 Cor. 1:3–7)

Those who become stuck are unintentionally blinded by tunnel vision. Their pain has caused them to focus inward. They are trying to survive and don't see the pain of those around them. Those who *don't* become stuck see their suffering for what it is and know that God is allowing it because He wants to use it for something greater. Those who are resilient *intentionally* use their suffering to better position themselves to comfort others. Suffering doesn't simply end with suffering. "Otherwise," as my colleague Boone says, "our suffering would simply be tragic." Suffering's end is purpose. Yes, *you* can experience purpose in *your* suffering. In the death of your loved one, your divorce, that traumatic event you wouldn't have wished on anyone, that unthinkable horror you weren't sure you'd survive. There is nothing you've experienced that God cannot, or will not, use purposefully.

We then should anticipate daily our purpose. One who suffers well looks closely at what is happening around them, seeking to discover how their pain can be used positively in the lives of others. Once we begin to cooperate with God, not much effort is required of us to discover how our situation can be used for His will, for others are in pain everywhere we look. This process is God's design; it changes our worldview as well as our view of our specific experience of suffering. The following are more stories of people who allowed their hurt to count for something good.

Paul

If you're curious about other purposeful heroes in Scripture, then a look at the New Testament is in order. Again, we'll turn to the apostle Paul. Paul had a shady history; he wasn't the best guy. In fact, he was downright cruel and hateful toward Christians. When he made a radical choice and submitted to God, he also invited persecution. Perhaps the same kind of persecution he'd shoveled out in the years prior. Paul was also repeatedly imprisoned. During one of those imprisonments, as recorded in Acts 27, he was transported on a ship that became caught up in a powerful northeaster. In the midst of this storm, Paul's resilience shown bright. After an angel appeared to him with a promise that the ship would wreck but all on board would survive, Paul boldly communicated that truth to those on the ship. Paul had already gained credibility with those who were given the task of guarding him. They knew his struggles, and they also saw that he was suffering in this new circumstance. They had grown to trust and respect him, and eventually the crew and passengers took orders from none other than the prisoner himself.

Our struggles give us credibility. Suffering positions us to be used for God's remarkable purpose. Paul was positioned by God and used by God. So was Esther. Can you imagine what it was like for each of them to experience God using them so powerfully? Did that fruit erase their pain? Certainly not. But the fruit reframed their pain in a profound way. Purpose changed the meaning of their suffering. It allowed them to process their struggles more healthily, and with great hope. The same can be true for you and for me. Purpose does not negate our suffering, but it will reframe it. How incredibly healing is a genuinely reframed hurt!

Frank

Frank is a dear colleague who has lived a full life. He knows both the experience of pain and the experience of the American dream. Frank was once a high school dropout washing buses in New York City. Then he went back to school for his GED, completed college and graduate school, and ultimately finished his career as the assistant commissioner of transportation for the New York City Department of Transportation, under the assignment of Rudy Giuliani. Frank understands the meaning of succeeding against the odds. You see, as a young boy, Frank endured significant abuse. He was hospitalized because of physical abuse and still today has no feeling in two of his fingers due to a violent attack by his father. Frank himself became violent in his teens and twenties. In his thirties, he had an encounter with God that changed his life. This experience changed him at his core and facilitated a journey of healing and purpose in his life. But, unfortunately, pain will always be part of life. Frank later experienced the tragic death of his son in a motorcycle accident.

Thankfully, Frank did not get stuck in the suffering that easily could have immobilized him. Frank doesn't rely on superficial coping skills that only invite additional, unnecessary suffering. Frank lives life with an eternal perspective, and he thrives when God allows him to use his painful past to help others. When he reflects on the burial of his son, a time that was especially challenging for him, he acknowledges that "it was tough to physically leave him at that gravesite. He was such a blessing in my life." But immediately following the burial, he determined within himself, "I'm going to see how God uses this for His glory." And, indeed, he has. Frank is a pastoral counselor who has spent the latter years of his life full of purpose, generously allowing others to benefit from the fruits of his sufferings. He has been an instrument in assisting others who have endured abuse, in healing marriages, and in ministering to those who grieve. Frank lives 1 Peter 4:19: "So then, those who suffer according to God's will should commit themselves to their faithful Creator and continue to do good." Frank is an amazingly resilient man who has learned to live well in his suffering.

Jeff

Jeff worked a stressful and dangerous job with federal law enforcement for many years. He was good at what he did and had earned the respect of many of his colleagues. Unfortunately, he had also become the target of a few criminals who had been negatively impacted by his perseverance. One person in particular strove for years to make Jeff's life miserable, communicating repetitive, graphic death threats to Jeff and his family. Jeff, his wife, and his children suffered intensely during this time. They lived in legitimate fear and experienced many measurable symptoms as the result of traumatic stress.

Jeff would be the first to tell you he didn't always cope well with his struggles. Indeed, both he and his wife endured intense battles with PTSD. They found the suffering to be nearly unbearable for a season but now have discovered the healing that results from using the experience of their trials to minister to others. Jeff eventually retired from federal law enforcement. In a turn of events that only God could have masterminded, Jeff is now the manager of chaplain development and ministry relations for the Billy Graham Rapid Response Team. He is responsible for the crisis training and development of sixteen hundred volunteer chaplains throughout the country. He travels around the world responding to national and international natural disasters and critical incidents of mass violence, training others in how to prevent and address the symptoms of PTSD and how to make sense of their suffering. Jeff will graciously tell you that God had to qualify him for the job, referring to the suffering he endured that enables him to succeed in his current role.

Jeff's willingness to allow God to use his pain purposefully has aided in his healing and developed in him a resilience that has positioned him to be emotionally and spiritually stronger than he was before his traumatic season began. Jeff's struggle is not entirely over, and it won't be as long as his offender is alive, but Jeff is proof that our circumstances don't have to be fully resolved for resilience to be present. Friends, this is what bouncing back looks like. And it's nothing short of beautiful!

Strengths + Suffering = Purpose

Maybe you are reading this today, and you feel inspired. You too desire for God to use your pain purposefully. But how? It is quite simple, actually. Despite your suffering, you have talents, gifts, and abilities, right? Maybe they are a bit dusty due to a season of discouragement, but they are still there. Now marry those strengths with your greatest point of pain, and you have a beautiful formula for purpose. *Strengths + Suffering = Purpose*

What does that formula look like in real-life terms? Let me give you a few examples:

1. A gifted pastor with a history of childhood sexual abuse uses his terrible experience to educate and more effectively minister to his parishioners who have suffered the same kind of abuse.

2. A woman who easily connects with children and was once abused by her husband volunteers to provide childcare in a shelter for survivors of domestic violence.

3. A widowed man with the gifts of mercy and compassion leads a support group related to grief.

4. A woman with the gift of hospitality who lost her child to cancer serves as a greeter at a special luncheon hosted for grieving mothers.

5. A wise businessman who experienced the trauma of divorce offers financial coaching to those who are adjusting to the financial challenges of separation.

6. A teen with a gift for writing whose mother spent years in prison writes notes of encouragement to other children whose parents are imprisoned.

7. An introverted woman who thrives in one-on-one relationships and also battled a decade-long addiction to drugs mentors and encourages another female to overcome her drug addiction.

8. A gifted public speaker who has suffered many health issues teaches a class on nutrition.

9. A happily married couple whose marriage survived bankruptcy reaches out to another couple after the husband receives a pink slip from his employer.

10. A retired talented carpenter who previously lost his home to a tornado provides practical reconstruction help to those who have lost their homes to natural disasters.

Obviously, there are no limits to how God can use our suffering to produce something beautiful. His creativity has no restrictions. Our job is to be willing and available for Him to use us. If this chapter pulls at your heartstrings, then your next step is to simply submit. *Submit* your hurt to God and be willing for Him to use you if and when He desires. (No need to panic. God is probably not calling you to speak to audiences across the country about your greatest pains. He is far more creative than that.) Then *anticipate* and be alert daily to opportunities. Next, it's time to *act*. It's time to allow your hurt to be used for a greater purpose. Respond to opportunities. Lastly, enjoy the *reward*. God provides an extra layer of healing and joy when we allow Him to use something so uncomfortable in our lives to yield something so beautiful when we give back to others in a positive way.

Your Platform

Everyone faces difficult circumstances. And everyone has an audience. Yes, even you. Whether we are on a mountaintop or in a valley, people are always watching us. We are an example to others. As my friend Patty has reminded me, "We have to teach them how to suffer. We teach how to die, how to have the promise of eternal life, but we also have to teach them how to be alive." Friend, your suffering is a platform and through it you can show others how to suffer well. In fact, your valley may just be the most powerful stage you have ever stepped on—so thank God for it. Without that stage, your suffering would simply be a tragedy. *For such a time as this . . .* Maybe this is *your* time, and the marriage of your strengths and your suffering is the platform God will use. *Submit. Anticipate. Act.* Your pain has taken so much away from you. What more do you have to lose? God will not waste your platform as long as you let him work through you and your circumstances.

Victory Verse

Praise be to the God and Father of our Lord Jesus Christ, the Father of compassion and the God of all comfort, who comforts us in all our troubles, so that we can comfort those in any trouble with the comfort we ourselves receive from God.

2 Corinthians 1:3–4

Application Questions

1. This final chapter offers insight into how to position ourselves so we give back to others—for our pain to produce fruit. This is the climax of resilience. What is your reaction to this challenge?

2. Ponder the formula *Strengths + Suffering = Purpose.* Consider some of your past or present spiritual heroes. How do you see evidence of this formula in their lives? How does this realization encourage you in your struggles?

3. Allowing our suffering to be used productively involves a series of steps:

Submit

Anticipate

Act

How are you doing regarding these steps? Have you submitted your suffering to God for His purpose? Are you acting on opportunities that you see? If you answered no to any of these questions, what hinders you?

4. If you are presently allowing God to guide you through the steps listed above, what rewards have you experienced? How is this purposeful use of your pain aiding in your healing?

5. What do you consider to be your greatest struggles? Did you know that those pains are positioning you for purpose?

6. Spiritual heroes are those who embrace purpose, and they don't just have to be people of the past. This is your time, and God wants to use anything and everything in your life for His greater purpose. How do you want to look back on your season of suffering? How do you want others to look back on it?

Don't allow your suffering to simply be a great tragedy. Embrace the opportunity to be made beautiful in a manner that only God, through His purpose, can accomplish. It's time to allow your struggles to take the stage!

CONCLUSION

When I hear the word *resilience*, I immediately think of a bouncy ball. I know that's not a very sophisticated image, but hear me out. When you throw a bouncy ball onto the floor, it bounces back higher than its starting point. When the ball first hits the floor, it is compressed and changes slightly in shape. Then it springs forward with power and restores its shape. The harder you throw it down, the higher it bounces in reaction. The resilience of the ball defies gravity.

Can it be so with our hurts in life as well? Is it possible for our tragedies to propel us to bounce back? Could we ultimately spring back in better shape than we were before we were slammed to the ground? Absolutely! And I've seen evidence of this resilience thousands of times within the quiet walls of my office. Friend, you too can bounce back. I know you can, because I know the God Who can lead you to resilience!

Of course, God works according to His timeline, not ours. He is a process-oriented healer, walking us *through* our hurts and our healing rather than around them or away from them. Will you trust Him to begin taking you through your pain? It's time to bounce back. Give yourself the privilege of that opportunity. Just because you've been stuck doesn't mean you have to stay there. Just as He did with Esther and Paul and all of the friends I've introduced you to in this book, God will bring blessings out of your curses. He wants you to bounce back.

Your hurts do not have to define you or dictate your future. Maybe your hurt occurred years ago, but you've lived with the residual effects for much of your life. You don't have to wait for eternity to find healing. Restoration can begin today, starting now. When you are stuck in your suffering, you cannot move beyond survival mode. You don't have the chance to fully live your life. But it is time now to live! To thrive! To heal! It is time to take your life back. Perhaps God has led you to this book for this very reason. He desires for you to bounce back from the hurt that has been robbing you and shrinking your world. Indeed, He has good plans for you (see Jer. 29:11). He desires to use your suffering to create something amazing. To benefit you. To propel you to even greater heights. Because He loves you, he wants to strengthen your resilience. He desires to use your hurt to create something beautiful in you, like the incredible transformation of a caterpillar to a butterfly.

Let us move forward with the instruction of James 1:2–6 as our guide:

> Consider it pure joy, my brothers and sisters, whenever you face trials of many kinds, because you know that the testing of your faith produces perseverance. Let perseverance finish its work so that you may be mature and complete, not lacking anything. If any of you lacks wisdom, you should ask God, who gives generously to all without finding fault, and it will be given to you. But when you ask, you must believe and not doubt, because the one who doubts is like a wave of the sea, blown and tossed by the wind.

These verses present a wonderful summary for our conclusion. Let's take a look at the four steps of instruction provided in these five verses of intense wisdom.

1. Lean in to your suffering, joyously looking forward to the fruits of maturity, completion, perseverance, and wholeness. Be careful of destructive thoughts that prevent this willing mind-set. Watch to make sure you do not add additional, unnecessary suffering as a result of being stuck.

2. Remember that what God starts He finishes to completion. Be careful of destructive theology that prevents you from embracing the true character of God. Also embrace an eternal perspective on pain. You can trust Him with your pain and suffering.

3. Remember that you will need wisdom during your seasons of pain, which God will provide freely when you ask. He will graciously give it without judgment or condemnation. Strive not to live an isolated life apart from God and the appointed people He uses to guide you along. Also be willing to incorporate the practical tools He provides that aid in building resilience.

4. Lastly, believe Him. Push away the doubts that hinder you, and watch as God accomplishes the impossible and rebuilds what is broken.

You do not need to fear suffering. You can abide in the One who promises the strength to endure. If you've been thrown to the ground, get ready to stand. Get ready to rise above your pain. Your suffering doesn't have to cripple you anymore! In fact, it can propel you to the heights of joy and purpose.

I hope you have already started your healing voyage, and I cannot wait to hear your story of resilience. You are becoming a hero in suffering. And Lord knows we could sure use some more heroes.

Thanks for joining me in the journey,
Donna

NOTES

Chapter 3 Why Staying Stuck Is Unhealthy

1. Don Colbert, MD, *Deadly Emotions: Understand the Mind-Body-Spirit Connection That Can Heal or Destroy You* (Nashville: Thomas Nelson, 2006), 211.

Chapter 4 Acknowledge the Suffering

1. "Toddler Trapped in a Texas Well Cries and Sings as Rescuers Dig," *New York Times*, October 16, 1987, http://www.nytimes.com/1987/10/16/us/toddler-trapped-in-a-texas-well-cries-and-sings-as-rescuers-dig.html.

Chapter 6 Consider a Different Angle

1. Joni Eareckson Tada, lecture, American Association of Christian Counselors World Conference, Nashville, TN, September 23, 2015.

2. Dr. Caroline Leaf, *Switch on Your Brain: The Key to Peak Happiness, Thinking, and Health* (Grand Rapids: Baker Books, 2015), 55–70.

Chapter 8 Maintain Healthy Relationships

1. Tom Rodgers and Bev Rodgers, *Becoming a Family that Heals: How to Resolve Past Issues and Free Your Future* (Colorado Springs: Focus on the Family, 2009).

2. Maija Reblin and Bert N. Uchino, "Social and Emotional Support and Its Implication for Health," *Current Opinion in Psychiatry* 21, no. 2 (March 2008): 201–5, http://doi.org/10.1097/YCO.0b013e3282f3ad89.

Chapter 9 Practice Self-Care

1. To learn more about Timothy and his ongoing ministry to the Muslim world, visit Timothyabraham.org.

2. "Stress Relief from Laughter? It's No Joke," Mayo Clinic, accessed March 8, 2017, http://www.mayoclinic.org/healthy-lifestyle/stress-management/in-depth/stress-relief/art-20044456?pg=1.

Donna Gibbs is a Licensed Professional Counselor Supervisor, a National Certified Counselor, and a Board Certified Professional Christian Counselor. A member of the American Association of Christian Counselors, she is on the referral network for Focus on the Family, Christian Care Network, r3Continuum, and FINDINGbalance. A Christian counselor since 1998, she is director of A Clear Word Counseling Center and of marriage and support ministries for Mud Creek Baptist Church in Hendersonville, North Carolina. She and her husband, Mark, have been married for more than twenty years and have four sons.

You can live free from anxiety

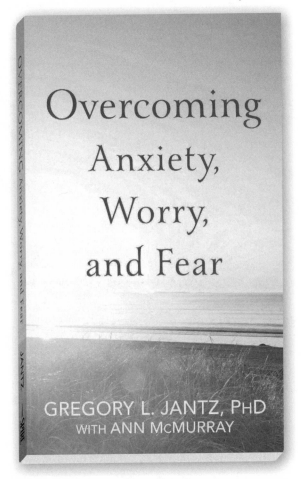

With compassion, common sense, and biblical wisdom, Dr. Jantz will help you identify the causes of your anxiety, assess the severity of your symptoms, and start down avenues for positive change.